MW00487788

INNOVATIVE
Women
IN HEALTHCARE

SUCCESS THROUGH EXCEPTIONAL LEADERSHIP

DR. EMILY LETRAN
DR. ALLISON HOUSE | AMY WOOD | DR. LAILA HISHAW
DR. HOA NGUYEN | DR. VI HO | DR. JONELLE GRANT ANAMELECHI
QUYEN LE | KRYSTYLLE RICHARDSON

INNOVATIVE *Women* IN HEALTHCARE

Quantity sales special discounts are available on quantity purchases by corporations, associations, and others. For details, contact the publisher at the address above.

Orders by U.S. and Canada trade bookstores and wholesalers. Email info@ BeyondPublishing.net

The Beyond Publishing Speakers Bureau can bring authors to your live event. For more information or to book an event contact the Beyond Publishing Speakers Bureau speak@BeyondPublishing.net

The Author can be reached directly at info@BeyondPublishing.net

Manufactured and printed in the United States of America distributed globally by BeyondPublishing.net

BEYOND
PUBLISHING

New York | Los Angeles | London | Sydney

ISBN Hardcover: 978-1-637921-71-5

ISBN Softcover: 978-1-637921-76-0

MARK VICTOR HANSEN
Author "Chicken Soup For The Soul"

As the author of" Chicken Soup for the Soul" and "Ask: The Bridge from Your Dreams to Your Destiny,"

I am excited about the book by Dr. Emily Letran, "Innovative Women in Healthcare: Success Through Exceptional Leadership."

This collection of stories and strategies from different leaders in different parts of healthcare will change your life and the way you do business.

Leadership has got to be innovative. It's got to have great impact, to create and innovate and change. This book helps you maximize your time and develop passive income. The stories help you transform from good to phenomenally good.

And if you need a key story to get you going, read my friend, Dr. Emily Letran's story. "Leaders Create Leaders."

"Innovative Women in Healthcare" is going to make your life infinitely better. I strongly recommend and endorse my friend, Dr. Emily Letran's book to you.

DR. ROBERT PICK

As one who has been around the block more than twice, who has also made every mistake more than once, and is not wanting anyone to make the mistakes I have made, this book is a must-read! It is also what I call "Super-Coolio-Awesome," and hence a BIG "Purple-Cow-Wow!"

Although it is written from a woman's point of view (so important), it applies to all, especially from its amazing motivational perspective. Reading this will also help you find your passion, your joy in life, and it will empower you make the right choices for the right reasons.

One of the authors talks about Dream Big! Yep – one of my own quotes, "Dream Big! Always shoot for another solar system and if you land on Saturn that is OK!" Well, *Innovative Women in Medicine/For Impact and Profits* will take you there!

Robert M. Pick, DDS, MS, FACD, FICD
CEO/Progressive Periodontics & Implants
CEO/The Pick Group

TABLE OF CONTENTS

FOREWORD

Dr Emily Letran has done an excellent job bringing together the stories of a fascinating group of female healthcare professionals. Their stories are both inspirational and educational. Each story is unique and helps the reader see that the road to success and fulfillment comes in many forms and that we have the ability to write our own stories.

Through their journeys and experiences, we see that the road can sometimes be bumpy, filled with obstacles and detours but if we are determined we can succeed. It is a very interesting read!

Maxine Feinberg DDS
Past President, American Dental Association

INNOVATIVE

omen

IN HEALTHCARE

CHAPTER 1

LEADERS CREATE LEADERS:
TOUCHING LIVES FOR GLOBAL IMPACT

Dr. Emily Letran

"The job of a leader today is not to create followers. It is to create more leaders."
Ralph Nader

I was born in war-torn Viet Nam and came to the U.S. as a refugee at the age of 13.

Before that, I lived with my parents, who were both philosophy teachers. I learned the value of knowledge and the respect for the truth from them, even if it meant being the contrarian. They were not allowed to teach their subjects after the Communist takeover and now, more than four decades later, my dad's students still share stories of him teaching ideas outside the approved book. I recognized at a very young age the value and importance of having a strong opinion and being able to influence others from a position of authority.

When my mother passed away in her late 30's due to cancer, I was the big eight-year-old sister to my younger siblings, including my little cousins in our extended family. I assigned these kids all of their household chores, along with teaching them how to read and write at home. At school, I was "naturally" appointed as the class leader because of my good grades. I remember feeling frustrated because the other kids simply could not "follow the rules," like boys needing to tuck in their shirts or girls stopping their chatting once class start. As a young leader, I learned to encourage my friends to follow the rules and set examples because we were one of the "model" classes for the whole school.

In 1981, when I was 13 years old, I left my father and two younger siblings to escape from Communist Viet Nam with my aunt. That was the first time I realized that sometimes you'd have to break the rules to achieve what you want. Our tiny little boat was shot at, stopped, and robbed by the Vietnamese Coast Guard. When they finally let us go, our journey continued on for seven more days, even though we ran out of food after the second day. We reached the refugee camp with everyone exhausted.

In the camp, I had the opportunity to witness the true spirit of humanity. Some of the refugees had survived severe trauma and hardship, yet were able to celebrate moments of joy with very little material possession. They held religious gatherings. They held parties when someone was accepted to go to the "third country," because it would be the end of their stay in the refugee camp, which could sometimes last for years. Some refugees in the camp saw the hard time of survival as a transition to a brighter future, though filled with uncertainty. However, the majority of the people regretted the journey, longed for the happier times in the past, and struggled with self-doubt.

Years later, I realized that in the face of challenges, we can either give in or face the challenge head on. When opportunity knocks, we have to be ready to grab and leverage it. Being different in your thinking, mindset, and determination will set you apart from others around you. This is part of your development of a leader.

In hindsight, I realize I was different than many of my colleagues from the very beginning of my dental career. I took over a small three-chair practice and within a short period of time decided on drastic action: we removed the lunch room to add the fourth operatory and a panoramic-cephalometric x-ray to accommodate two specialists in the already-crowded office. The addition immediately relieved the overbooked schedule, and we soon outgrew the space. We moved two more times within the next few years to embrace growth rather than being content with where we were.

Over a period of six years, I also bought and sold four practices. That journey included real estate acquisitions, demolitions, build outs, and a whole host of other projects I had to learn on my own, besides running my professional practice business. I was driven by the ambition of growth. I learned later that a leader should have that vision of growth, of beginning with the end in mind, of moving the team to action, and of seeing the opportunity and potential when others may not.

"If you want to go fast, go alone.
If you want to go far, go together."
African Proverb

A leader can only do so much on his or her own. In order to be successful, the leader should leverage the knowledge of experts and empower others to help.

I remember my earlier days as a business owner. Instead of trying to learn everything, I studied the experts in growth in my dental space. I invested in 30 VHS tapes teaching "30-Day Dental MBA" by Dr. Howard Farran. I specifically read "The Profitable Dentist" newsletter by Dr. Woody Oaks and "The Richards Report" by Doctors Richard Madow and David Madow. These resources helped expedite my learning because they taught the golden nuggets of business success.

My mentality was to make business easier, faster, and more fun. As I grew, I empowered my staff to grow also. I would invest in traveling for seminars as a whole team despite the fact I have "HMO offices" that are not supposed to be profitable by industry myths. We went to Vegas, Cancun, Hawaii, Alaska, learning, growing, and having fun together. The team leaders emerged as they saw my vision to grow and have fun together. Creating leaders was the biggest "secret" in growing the business. You can duplicate yourself with associates. You cannot grow until you have leaders who want to grow with you, to step up and "earn" more responsibility, and to cherish the milestones the business attains as well as what they achieve in their personal lives.

"If your actions inspire others to learn more, dream more, do more, and become more, you are a leader." John Quincy Adams

During the early days of my career, while my colleagues were focusing on clinical training through extensive continuum, I invested in business, marketing, and personal development programs. I realized understanding business is a key to creating the life I wanted, whether it was having a solo practice or being able to leverage other associates and have more time to spend with my family. I knew it was important to make sure the people who love and support me most – my family – understand and appreciate what I do, even if they did not participate in the business.

The focus on personal growth and business systems helped me grow three successful dental group practices with very small, efficient staffs, leveraging the talents of associate doctors and specialists.

Instead of creating lots of rules, I set up guidelines and empowered the staff to grow with incentivized goals, based on business metrics. Employees grow when they feel appreciated, and they often enjoy being challenged at work instead of following regular routines. Rather than spending money on material things like fancy cars and expensive vacations, I invested in trainings for my teams. My staff knew they were expected to improve their performance with tracking goals. Our patients are often impressed with the trips our team took together because we achieved business goals. We went on an Alaskan cruise, visited Cancun *cenote*, watched fancy Vegas shows, and worked super-hard when we were in the office. My staff received a "raise" as a bonus every year, not based on the industry norm of seniority, but based on great performances.

"The greatest leader is not necessarily the one who does the greatest things. He is the one that gets the people to do the greatest things."

Ronald Reagan

Many years ago, I worked as an associate and made friends with several dental assistants. One of them, Jenny, really enjoyed working with me. Besides the daily work of general dentistry, we were both challenged every Friday because that was the day dedicated to children's dentistry, when we might do sedation on young patients and efficiently complete full mouth treatments. I remember missing lunches on those kids' days because we were expected to work straight through, taking care of patients who came in ready for sedation.

When I bought my first practice, I asked Jenny to come and help me. She stayed for many years, learning new skills including orthodontics, which is a specialty I required all my staff to learn. She moved on to manage a specialist office, started her family and had two children.

One day, I got a call from her. "Dr Letran, I'm calling to let you know my husband and I just bought a house!"

"Congratulations!" I said.

She continued, "You are the first person I am sharing this news with! I have not even told my mom."

"I'm so grateful you'd do that for me. Why?"

I teared up as she told me, "I wanted to share this good news with you first because you always encouraged us to do more and achieve more for ourselves and our families. I am a better person because of you."

Years later, I realized I have that gift – the gift to inspire and move people to action. When I coach my clients, I help them understand their goals very clearly and I have that "touch" to encourage them to step up and step into their own power.

One of my clients, Dr. Sandra, had done extensive training in cosmetic dentistry and decided to host hands-on workshops. By the time she shared this project with me, she had already invited a cosmetic guru from another country to come and teach the class. "Why don't you teach the class yourself?" I asked.

"I'm not an expert; I'm not famous," she answered.

I painted a picture of reality for her: "You have done the continuum, the training, the certification. You spent years perfecting the craft. You have a practice focused on cosmetic dentistry. You are qualified to teach."

Our gift as leaders is to see the potential in others and invite them to grow. I am especially proud about the accomplishments of Dr. Sandra. She went on to host and teach her own seminar series, helping other dentists change their practices and their lives.

As I helped others grow, I decided to share my knowledge and expertise in accelerating business success by dedicating my time to help other business professionals with my coaching and consulting programs. An expert is usually a speaker who can train and teach. As a newbie in the speaking world, I found myself constantly seeking opportunities to present my talk, and of course, I chose to serve across all industries.

The desire to be a leader inherently led me to host my own live events, although I had no previous experience! As a practicing dentist for almost three decades who had never been on any stage, several years ago I started to host my own radio show and held my signature event ACTION To WIN across the US and in multiple countries, attracting industry leaders as collaborators in addition to larger corporate sponsors. As a leader active on multiple platforms, I am blessed to be able to connect with other business owners and help them grow with the right mindset and action plan of a leader.

I believe when your desire and passion present that calling for you to be a leader, you should answer it. You should ask for help, and the universe will present options for you. My journey from a Vietnamese refugee to a healthcare professional speaking on international stages and featured in Forbes was not an accident. It was the result of strategy, intention, expert guidance, and the desire to inspire and grow others as leaders.

I know my colleagues in healthcare will see little parts of themselves in my story. I hope to be the catalyst to help them accelerate and achieve all of their dreams, in business and in life.

DR. EMILY LETRAN

Dr. Emily Letran is a serial entrepreneur, CEO of multiple dental practices, and private coach to many professionals. As an international speaker, she has been on TEDx and shared stages with countless business leaders including Sharon Lechter (Co-Author of Rich Dad Poor Dad), Dan Clark (Hall of Fame Speaker), Dr. Howard Farran (Dental Town), and Linda Miles (The Ultimate Mentor of Dentistry). She has been featured in several magazines including Dental Town , Global Woman, and See Beyond as well as other media: Yahoo!Finance, Forbes, USA Today, and FOX. She is a contributing writer for Dental IQ, DrBicuspid.com, and Dentistry Today. Dr Letran is the Founder of Exceptional Leverage Inc., host of ACTION To WIN seminars, author of several books, and a Certified Kolbe Consultant, helping teams grow with customized insights to boost performance. She can be reached regarding speaking, guest expert appearances, high-performance coaching, consulting and marketing strategist at: emily@exceptionalleverage.com

Or call 323-484-4989.

www.AmericanDreamCoach.com

www.linkedin.com/in/coachemilyletran

Text action2021 to 26786 for your High-Performance Assessment

Book a 30-Minute Focus Call:

www.calendly.com/coachemilyletran

CHAPTER 2

"I NEVER SAID IT WOULD BE EASY..."

Dr. Allison House

"...I only said it would be worth it." In my mind, I only heard my dad's voice saying these familiar words as the announcer's voice boomed over the loudspeaker.

"Allison House, first attempt!"

In December 1994, I was competing in the USA Weightlifting American Open in Flagstaff, Arizona, representing the club Olympic weightlifting team of Northern Arizona University, where I was in the first semester of my senior year. The venue was bracingly cold. Flagstaff in the middle of winter often sees days that barely get above freezing, and that day was no different. With the doors to the room repeatedly opening and closing, that chill permeated the event.

With my one minute on the clock to make a lift, my coach – who was also my father – pulled me aside and gave me some advice. I was expecting technical cues or some great pep talk, but what he told me was that "it didn't matter." In all honesty, in that moment, those words were something of a letdown. But what he explained next was that I was only to focus on myself, not on the American record holder who was warming up in the back, the past and future Olympians in the audience, or what anyone else was doing that day. I was not to focus on what I had lifted in the past, or what I might lift in the future. "Do the best you can, right now, and everything else will be fine."

I made the lift. I did not win the competition – not even close – but I made the lift I needed to make to give my team the much-needed points. Interestingly, his advice was sage. Winning that competition was not important. In fact, most people have no idea that I ever lifted weights at all. What was important was training hard to perform the best I could and having the courage to get out onto a platform – where all eyes are on you and only you – and attempt something difficult. Knowing that I did the best I could meant that I could live with the result and there was no voice in my head whispering that I should have done better. I also learned other valuable lessons from weightlifting, perhaps the most important of which is that if you want to be good, really good, you have to have the courage to step out of your comfort zone and live your life in a manner that supports that goal.

After NAU, my husband and I moved to Atlanta, Georgia, where he was attending Emory University School of Law. I had planned on going to medical school, but my father had been diagnosed with throat cancer in 1994. He was diagnosed by our family dentist, who saved my father's life by catching the cancer early enough for treatment to be successful. That inspired me to become a dentist, so I spent the year in Atlanta working and applying to dental schools. The night before I was to take the Dental Admission Test, Hurricane Opal ravaged Atlanta. The next morning, we had no power and a huge tree had fallen across the only street in and out of our neighborhood. I ended up walking to the exam center, which, thank goodness, had power.

Nonetheless, I matriculated into the University of Alabama at Birmingham in the fall of 1996.

I grew up in Flagstaff, which at the time had a population of about 45,000 people, and relocating to the southern United States was a huge change for me. Moving by myself to Birmingham, Alabama (my husband was still in Atlanta attending law school) was tough. I was entering a class where only 11 of my fellow students were female and joining a profession that was still very male-dominated. As luck would have it, my Olympic weightlifting background, as well as my bachelor's degree in math had prepared me well for being part of a male-dominated class. As one would expect, I learned a lot about both dentistry and life from my colleagues and professors in dental school. One of the statements that really resonated with me was a particular professor who said, quite boldly, "I'm good because I want to be good." He was a top-notch clinician who always tried to reach the best possible outcome and always strove to make his work better.

In the summer before my second year of dental school, I became pregnant with my son. It wasn't an ideal time to have a baby! My husband had another year left of law school in Atlanta which is three-hour drive away. He graduated and moved to Alabama six weeks after my son was born. It felt like I was alone during that time, but I wasn't. My classmates at UAB that year were there throughout the whole thing. They were wonderful to me and I will forever be grateful for the support and kindness they showed me during that challenging time.

The baby was due in late March – in the middle of the semester. When I approached my professors to let them know, I was given two options – repeat the year, or miss no more than a week of class and continue.

I had a c-section on a Tuesday and was back in class the following Monday. I learned at that time that it really does take a village to be successful in life – a lesson that informs much of how I treat those around me even now. For six weeks after I had my son, a classmate brought me dinner each night. Most of my classmates had never held a baby, but pretty much every one of them held my son that semester so I could take a test or wax up a case.

This is probably why I always assume the best in all dentists. There have been rare occasions when it turned out that a dentist was actually a bad person, but, for the most part, dentists are incredibly kind and generous people who just want to do good work.

My husband moved to Birmingham after he graduated in May of 1998. After we had another baby during my fourth year of dental school, I graduated from UAB School of Dentistry and we all moved to Phoenix, Arizona.

My husband and I had numerous discussions as we were driving across the country in our moving truck. One of the more salient points in one discussion was an agreement that we would always do the right thing. In both of our professions, there are infinite opportunities to take advantage of the fact that we have superior knowledge to those we are serving. Always doing the right thing sometimes comes at a cost, both in terms of earnings and in terms of ego. It was an agreement that we have kept, although it hasn't always been easy.

When I arrived in Arizona, I worked in a variety of dental practices, some good, some bad, but none that were the caliber that I wanted to practice. In particular, I worked in one practice that was owned by a non-dentist. At the time, if something went wrong with a patient, the dentist's license (MY license) was on the line with the Arizona Board of Dental Examiners. The owner of the practice, as a non-dentist, had no responsibility for any problems at the office. I noticed that being an employee dentist working in a non-dentist owned practice means that you have little voice in treatment decisions, infection control, or billing, and yet are completely liable for these things.

I was eventually fired from that practice for refusing to extract an entire arch of teeth and seat a denture that had been made by an assistant. Many colleagues felt that I had no choice but to NOT deliver that denture. But I can tell you that my family was not amused by me getting fired when I had two kids in daycare, a mortgage, and student loans to pay. I feel for dentists put in the same position who don't have a professional spouse to cover them for a time.

I firmly believed that non-dentist owned practices were a significant problem, so I approached the Arizona Dental Association about the issue. I was invited to share my story at the Arizona Dental Association's House of Delegates. Later, I shared my story at the American Dental Association's House of Delegates. It was embarrassing, but I decided it was like weight lifting. I might fail and be ridiculed, but nothing would be gained if I didn't have the courage to go out and try. The end result was that the dentists in Arizona had the state pass legislation making non-dentist practice owners liable for the work that was being produced and gave employee dentists more agency in the process. The same resolution was passed as policy at the ADA level much later.

I was certainly not the first dentist to identify this problem, I was just the first one who was willing to stand up and speak about the issues. I learned another valuable lesson at that point – no one is coming to rescue you. If you want to make change, you cannot simply wait until someone else fixes it; you have to have the courage to initiate reforms. I had no idea what was going to happen when I raised this issue. I could have been blackballed and labeled a troublemaker for the rest of my career. But it was the right thing to do, and therefore the only option.

Soon after my speech in the Arizona Dental Association's House of Delegates, I was asked to become actively involved in organized dentistry. I was placed on the New Dentist Committee.

I opened my own practice from scratch in 2002. Doing the right thing is hard when you have bills to pay, but my practice philosophy was to put my patients first and perform only the treatment they actually need. As one might expect, there were a lot of lean years in the early days of my practice. I continued to strive to improve my work, sometimes at great personal cost.

In 2004, I had become the Chair of the New Dentist Committee for the Arizona Dental Association. I decided to create a continuing education (CE) course called "The Good, the Bad, and the Ugly." In truth, I did it for selfish reasons. I wanted to know how to talk to patients and how to get my work to be perfect EVERY SINGLE TIME. After all, this is the goal they taught me in dental school! The premise of the program was to present less-than-ideal cases in front of an audience with a panel of more experienced dentists to comment and recommend verbiage for discussion and suggestions for better treatment. Putting myself (and my work) on display to be openly criticized was hard, really hard, but I wanted answers. I was back to my weightlifting roots. The only way to get better is to have the courage to ask for guidance and then implement whatever advice the coach gave.

The advice given by the experienced dentists in this forum wasn't even close to what I thought. They helped me and all the other dentists in the room realize that sometimes you get a bad result despite your best efforts. My favorite quote was (and still is) "Your tooth broke my file." They had great verbiage to explain a bad outcome to a patient and how to present next steps. They were brilliant!

There ended up being a tremendous dialogue in that continuing education course, as members of the audience started sharing some of their own stories and asking what the panel would have done differently. The CE remains very popular and has been given many times over the years. I would like to believe that making myself vulnerable has improved the quality of dentistry and the lives of many young dentists by making it acceptable to recognize while we strive for excellence, we are not perfect.

I kept serving in organized dentistry and, several years after my term on the New Dentist Committee, I was assigned to serve as a delegate to the Arizona Dental Association's House of Delegates. This is the same body I had nervously spoken in front of years earlier.

At one meeting I asked a pointed question about the state association's budget. The budget presented had line items that made no sense to me. I am not an accountant and I was certainly afraid someone would mock me for asking a dumb question, but I had to ask. As it turns out, many of those line items were attempts to hide some misconduct. After asking a few too many more questions, I was nominated as the Treasurer for the Arizona Dental Association! I hadn't even served as treasurer on the local level, but I wanted to help put things right for our state dental association. I believed then, and still believe now, that transparency is key.

After my term as Treasurer ended, I was elected as President of the Arizona Dental Association. I was the youngest President ever and only the fourth woman to serve in that role. I started a Women in Dentistry group in Arizona during my tenure as President to create a safe place for women to address issues that are unique to being a female dentist.

My dad took issue with the Women in Dentistry group. In fact, many male dentists took issue with it. I understood. For many men, women's groups are about controlling men. From my dad's perspective, my mother's 1970s faculty wives club was only about getting my dad and his colleagues to pay attention to their spouses. The Women in Dentistry group was more about collaboration and idea-sharing that had nothing to do with our male colleagues. Being a woman dentist who owned her own practice and wanted to be a mom held unique challenges like maternity leave coverage, breast-feeding schedules, childcare issues and sick kids, in addition to the challenges of traveling alone to third world countries for needed CE.

I adore my male dentist colleagues. They have been nothing but kind and supportive of me (and I of them). That being said, they had no idea how to help me when I had a child home sick for a week with chicken pox. They couldn't relate when I was afraid to go to Haiti by myself for an implant placement course, and their wives were not on board for them to travel with me. It wasn't callous, they just had different challenges.

After my term as the Arizona Dental Association's state president, I was asked to participate in the American Dental Association's Success program. This was a program where dentists went and lectured a premade presentation to dental students across the country. One of the premade presentations was on ethics and it spoke to me. Oddly, other dentists on our ADA success team didn't like this presentation. In my opinion, ethics is all about courage. Courage to start a difficult conversation with a colleague or a patient. Courage to listen to patients without judgment and answer with kindness and compassion. Courage to admit to a bad outcome and offer solutions. Courage to honor the safe doctor-patient space and allow the truth to unfold, even when it is a criticism about you.

It is important to note that I am not a formally trained bio-ethicist, so my approach tends to be more practical in nature. Often, I use the wise words from my The Good, The

Bad, and The Ugly experience with the students. There isn't time in dental school to really think about the ethical issues that arise every day in practice, and I like to give students these skills.

I have been a delegate to the American Dental Association's House of Delegates for about 10 years now. I have moved into ADA leadership and I am currently serving on the ADA Council on Dental Practice. This has been eye-opening! The Council on Dental Practice writes policies for the nation's practice of dentistry. Policies must be approved by the American Dental Association's House of Delegates, and then they become the position of the American Dental Association. Policies include things like how sleep medicine should be practiced, how teledentistry should be done, and who should be allowed to place silver diamine fluoride. The policies are then used to make laws at the state level. Not all states follow the policies created by the ADA, but the policies make it easier to get laws passed that make sense to all dentists.

The Council also has its members sit in, listen, and comment on standards created by agencies like Digital

Imaging and Communications in Medicine (DICOM), to make sure they understand how they impact dental practices. Too often people who are not dentists will try and make rules that would cost a fortune to put into practice, such as forcing every dental practice to buy a medical diagnostic radiology quality monitor for every operatory.

When the COVID-19 pandemic started, I, along with everyone else, wanted clear guidance as to how to react. What precautions do we need to take? How do we treat emergencies? Can someone infected with COVID-19 be excluded from treatment? There were innumerable questions and no answers. This was truly when the lesson "no one is coming" sunk in for me. I am reminded of the scene from "Apocalypse Now" where, in the middle of a fire-fight, Martin Sheen's character asks a soldier, "Who's the commanding officer here, soldier?" and gets the response, "Ain't you?" There was no guidance from anywhere and everyone was looking to someone, anyone, who might have an answer on what we as dentists needed to do.

I was slated to do my ethics lecture for the Arizona Dental Association, dealing with the usual "I-got-an-untrue-

Yelp-review" type of situations and patient management problems. About a week before the lecture, I decided we needed something much more relevant to the pandemic.

I decided to take the moral philosophy principles I had developed and apply them to dentistry.

As it turns out, moral philosophy and ethics have gone hand in hand for centuries. It was easy to write the lecture. In truth, it is easy to see that the principles my father gave me about having the courage to step out and do something hard; the agreement my husband and I made about doing the right thing; the attitude of my professor that I am good because I want to be good; and the belief that all dentists are kind and generous people doing their best (from my UAB classmates) made teaching ethics a simple leap. Add in there the reality that I am in charge of my destiny (which I learned in organized dentistry); and that everyone deserves a little grace (which I learned from the Good, the Bad, and The Ugly); and you have the whole picture of me and what I stand for.

DR. ALLISON HOUSE

Dr. Allison House graduated from the University of Alabama – Birmingham. She is a private practice dentist in Phoenix, Arizona where she has her own solo practice. She began a long leadership run with Arizona Dental Association (AzDA) beginning as Chair of the New Dentists program through the Council on Membership. Dr. House moved up to AzDA Treasurer and then became one of AzDA's youngest, and most accomplished, Presidents. She is currently a speaker for the "ADA Success" program and serves on the ADA Council on Dental Practice. Dr. House is a Fellow of the International College of Dentists. She is married and the mother of two adult children.

CHAPTER 3

FROM BOSSY TO BOSS LADY

Amy Wood

"You're so bossy!" This was a phrase I heard constantly as a young girl. Being "bossy" meant finding myself in many different authoritative roles growing up, not knowing I was training myself for what life had in store for me. I volunteered to be in charge of group projects throughout my teenage years, and I gravitated toward jobs and tasks that had leadership opportunities as a young adult. Now, I have been blessed, and cursed, with three daughters that are bossy. The difference? I don't tell them they're being bossy; I tell them they are fostering and honing leadership skills, because girls can be bosses and leaders, too.

It's incredible how far we have come as a society in regards to women's rights, yet how far we have left to go.

A JOURNEY INTO DENTAL

Every job I have held has been healthcare-related in some aspect. I worked in a nursing home in high school, a surgical Intensive Care Unit in college, and I was a nanny for a dentist. Okay, that one is a bit of a stretch, but the correlation is there. My point is, healthcare has always been a big part of my life.

My life took a hard left in 2004 while I was a nanny, trying to figure out what to do next in life. I answered the door for my boss's IT professional, and there stood this skinny, geeky guy who was there to set up a backup of the dentist's patient database on their home computer. While this was cutting edge technology back in 2004, it's horrifying to admit now as a HIPAA and data breach consultant. This shy and oftentimes awkward guy swept me off my feet and I ended up marrying him.

Sadly, I found that his kind and generous nature was often taken advantage of in his profession and my protective tendencies kicked in. Before we were even married, I found myself answering phones, documenting what he did for clients and billing them - which was something he only occasionally did. Years later, I realized I pushed my way in and helped turn it into a proper business, rather than a hobby that (sometimes) paid the bills.

Running a small business with your significant other is not for everyone. By that, I mean it takes an extraordinary relationship to have so much togetherness. You must compartmentalize everything; your relationship, your feelings, your roles at both home and work, and above all, the way you speak to each other. All of this takes tremendous effort.

We learned together and began building our business as a team. Constructing a client list from word-of-mouth referrals is difficult under normal circumstances. Doing it for an IT business is even more arduous. Add to that the burden of your husband deciding to make you 51% owner of that business and putting you in charge of running everything – excruciating! I instantly regretted not taking more business classes in college. Instead, I learned on the job, which meant there were many painful missteps along the way. But we persevered, and with that, ACS Technologies, LLC was born, with me at the helm, for better or worse.

The good news was that I have thick skin and learn quickly. The bad news was that business, and especially the IT industry, can be cutthroat. I was raised to be brutally honest; however, honesty is often preyed upon in business situations. I learned quickly when to keep quiet and when to use silence as a tool. That's not to say I don't slip and offer my classic "punch in the throat" approach to communicating, but I like to think I've grown some over the years.

In 2013, things changed - again. Even though HIPAA, the Health Insurance Portability and Accountability Act, had been around since 1996, it did not get the attention or adherence it required. Then came the Omnibus Final Rule. This new addition supplemented the Security Rule and HITECH Act, which made IT Providers financially liable if we didn't offer security as part of our services.

The IT industry was starting to entertain the idea of Managed Services rather than "call us when it breaks." This meant the IT provider would have a contract with a client and provide certain managed services, such as anti-virus and backups. While the Managed Service Provider (MSP) concept was not revolutionary, we saw the possibilities and decided to embrace it.

I remember going to the Dental Integrators Association conference in 2013 and mentioning to a few members that we would be making this change. The concept was met with a resounding, "you're crazy." Yes, we were a bit crazy, but we were also in the perfect position to make the change. We had 75 dental, medical, and business clients that we considered actual customers. This meant we were small and agile enough to make such a significant change. It also provided a considerable pucker factor if it didn't work out.

We had catered to what our clients wanted us to do for far too long rather than what should have been done. When we embraced Managed Services as a model and looked at our clients as risks instead of revenue, we shifted the power back to us as the experts. However, everyone had their own computers, and they knew just enough to use the lingo and try to negotiate. As terrifying as it was, we drew a line in the sand and told our clients the world was moving in this direction, and we as a business were doing the same. Jump on the train or jump off, but there would be no in-between.

Being early adopters in anything is painful, but it could be life or death in your own small business. We often ask clients to refrain from being the guinea pigs or beta testers for new software versions because there is a difference between "cutting edge" and "bleeding edge." The bleeding edge hurts like hell.

Our bleeding-edge acceptance and encouragement for our clients to join us in compliance and security was excruciating. In a matter of five months, we went from 75 clients to 35. There were quite a few months where I honestly didn't know where the mortgage payment was coming from, but somehow, we made it through. We would get a new client, or someone would do a computer replacement project - something would happen - and we would squeak through another month until the panic started all over again. It was a roller coaster ride, and not a fun one.

We purchased expensive programs at a premium because we were small and had zero negotiating power. We added firewalls and encrypted email in addition to more costly and time-consuming anti-virus and backup programs. We had to learn new programs, manage vendors, budget appropriately, and continue to strive to change clients' and potential clients' minds on this new way of thinking.

As it turns out, the fee-for-service, or Break/Fix model, has a financial incentive for the provider to ensure a client is down for as long as possible. Why? It was the only way for the IT provider to rack up as much billable time as possible. When the client has no computer problems, the IT provider doesn't get paid. How backward is that?

Our Managed Service model is a fixed rate, but the financial incentive is the opposite. We make money when the practice or business is up and fully functional. When the products and services we resell for security and support make our job easier and quicker, we have less windshield time, the client gets back to production level work faster, and we both make a profit for a fixed price.

A JOURNEY INTO HIPAA

Then came the cherry on top of this tough business transition. After an already brutal year of implementing contracts, losing clients, hiring our first and second employees, along with a pregnancy (our third child), I got a letter in the mail.

It turns out that people do dumb things that affect others every day. That day in 2013 happened to be my turn to suffer. In 2011, I had orthognathic jaw realignment surgery on both upper and lower jaws. I had all kinds of issues, including the titanium screws unthreading themselves, which resulted in the titanium being removed over six months as new bone grew, but I digress.

The hospital across the street had recently purchased the imaging center where my X-rays were taken for the surgery. The hospital's internal IT department was transferring all the images. Having never worked with an IT department, the front desk person at the imaging center was nervous. According to the notification letter I received, she copied all the X-rays onto a thumb drive and supposedly "lost it." Unfortunately, my name, birthdate, social security number, and medical record number were all in plain text on these images. My identity had been compromised and later turned up on the dark web.

I felt violated.

The more I researched, the more confused I became. What was HIPAA? Can you re-issue an identity? What happens to the person that caused this damage? I had so many questions, so I got my hands on every piece of information I could. I had studied pre-law in college so I could figure this out, right? That is when I realized that the internet is full of people with their interpretations of "facts," which are often just loose suggestions. I wanted answers. I went to the federal register and downloaded all the laws. I spent weeks, and a box of highlighters, going through and figuring out what applied to us as an IT Provider and what applied to our clients.

This gave us additional reinforcement that choosing Managed Services as a long-term model was the right decision. Next, I put together a slide deck on our fancy first-generation iPad, and took that to every one of our clients to explain why we had been changing our offerings. I realized that if you have a reason, based on facts, for a change you are making, there is a lot less push back. Not none, but significantly less.

We are now on our third version of Managed Services contracts. It's nothing magical, and no secret sauce prevents our clients from being attacked by ransomware. Instead, it's good old-fashioned common sense and business security best practices.

Most people (normal people anyway) don't wake up and say, "Hey, ya know what sounds awesome? HIPAA! Government Regulation sounds amazing, and everyone will love me if I help them with it." Nope.

No one will say that ever, and what happens instead is a pivotal moment that changes the course of someone's career. For me, it was the compromise of my identity through dental x-rays. Looking back, I'm still a little upset, and also incredibly grateful for that data breach. Without it, I wouldn't be on this crazy business journey that has branched into multiple other unexpected, astounding, fantastic journeys full of equally surprising, remarkable, incredible experiences and people.

A JOURNEY INTO EDUCATION

That simple slide deck and conversation with our clients quickly turned into a class encompassing HIPAA privacy and security. Our clients wanted more. What else could I teach them? Could they get Continuing Education Units? After researching, I discovered HIPAA is unmistakably viable for Continuing Education Units. Unfortunately, the Dental Board of California, where all my clients were located at the time, did not have HIPAA listed as a required course. How is that possible?

Infection Control, OSHA, Bloodborne Pathogens, CPR, and California Dental Practice Act were all required, but not HIPAA. Never mind the fact it is a federal law that applies to dentists. Needless to say, the "bossy girl" in me didn't take that very well. After nine months of back and forth with the dental board, HIPAA became a core course due to its federal mandate for education. Score one for the lady with leadership skills!

Since then, we've added courses in HIPAA, Patient Privacy, Data Security, Cybersecurity, Data Breach Prevention, Technology Disaster Preparedness, and

California Dental Practice Act - including detecting abuse in patients and e-prescription requirements and guidance. We also expanded our education outside of California. We became licensed through the Academy of General Dentistry and the Dental Board of California to provide Continuing Education to all dental professionals nationally.

Educating people is one of my favorite things to do, and I don't mean boring education. I use pictures, tell stories, and rarely have more than a handful of words on slides. We've all sat through enough boring lectures where the educator reads the slides or uses legal and technical jargon that doesn't make sense to the average person. I realized fast that if I was going to do this, it would be practical, easy to understand, and have real examples that apply to dental practices. None of the multi-million-dollar fines for hospitals; my audience wouldn't relate. No one complies, especially in the HIPAA space, if they don't hear stories of their peers having issues with HIPAA and Cybersecurity.

While education remained a pivotal component to HIPAA Compliance, there was – and still is - so much more. Risk Analysis, Security Risk Assessment, Penetration

Testing - so many things I didn't want to get into at that time. I started searching for a vendor to partner with that I could refer my clients to.

I kept searching and searching, and I continue to explore to this day, although nothing seems to be in-depth enough - at least to my standards. I understand many programs claim to be all you need, but they were always left lacking after they went through my scrutiny. So, what did the woman who always looked for leadership opportunities do? I started building a complete HIPAA support program encompassing everything I was looking for end to end - education and paperwork, layered with IT security. It became our People, Process, Technology Program.

Then the calls started coming in to help with Data Breach Mitigation...

A JOURNEY INTO DATA BREACH CONSULTING

One day I got a frantic call from a dentist saying she got my number from a colleague that recently started working with us on HIPAA consulting. It turns out this dentist picked up my business card at a trade show six months prior but didn't call because she was too busy.

During Christmas break, someone took the door off its hinges at her practice and stole the unencrypted server. Fortunately, the backups were in another location, and the thieves didn't steal everything. Imagine walking into that chaos on a Monday morning after an extended holiday break. No wonder everyone, including the doctor, was panicking.

She took a chance on me, and I took a chance on her. Together we learned all the things NOT to do during a data breach, starting with notifying patients properly. Sending an email with generic information about a server theft is not appropriate. Sending a paper letter with that email message language is also not appropriate. Sending a long letter outlining what happened and how the patients can protect themselves - much better.

My role was to organize HIPAA-specific attorneys, vendors for computer forensics, notification letters, and credit monitoring. That's still a big part of what I do today, but truth be told, the biggest job I have is providing a shoulder to cry on, ears to listen, and hope that they can latch on to that there are better days ahead. In fact, when I start a data breach consultation, I ask what their favorite adult beverage is, and we sit down for a cocktail – or three. It's a painful, expensive journey, and I find that one cocktail gives a brief reprieve to clear the mind before the madness.

In that first data breach project the biggest hurdle was the existing IT guy. I went in wanting to preserve the IT relationship if possible. It quickly unraveled when the attorneys and I started asking questions about simple things like: "Why do you still have Windows XP computers? Why isn't the office using encrypted email for sending X-rays and treatment plans? What do you mean you don't believe in firewalls? Seriously, you put the computers on chunks of Styrofoam for 'flood control'?" I couldn't believe the words coming out of my mouth at certain times. This IT guy worked with many dental practices in the San Francisco Bay Area. Sadly, he ended up involved in over a dozen data breaches I got called in on. Surprisingly, he's still in business - and still doesn't believe in firewalls. Sometimes, you can't fix stupid.

In the end, the attorneys advised the dentist to terminate all engagement with the existing IT guy. They hired ACS Technologies, and we immediately installed a firewall. Physical security was implemented, including physically cabling the server to a wall inside a cage. The recently fired IT guy replaced the stolen server with an exact, unencrypted replica. When we replaced the server, the hard drives were pulled, wiped, and crushed appropriately. The server case sat in our office for a month until our next e-waste pickup. Every time I walked past it, I kicked it for causing me so much drama: it turns out everyone in our office took turns kicking it.

In the end, this doctor spent hundreds of thousands of dollars mitigating and remediating this stolen server. Yet, there were no fines, penalties, or patient lawsuits, and no patients left the practice. What did happen was the patients saw positive changes happening and the practice taking data security seriously. It went a long way and was a beautiful public relations campaign. The reason it worked is that the whole team believed in the outcome.

I still work with this office today. The doctor's daughter that referred me purchased it and merged it with her father's office; both are thriving. They are one of my favorite clients, not just because they get it and have embraced my program, but because they are genuinely lovely people. They deserve to have someone who has their back to help protect them from this or something worse from happening.

When the new location had an attempted break-in, no one freaked out because we knew the server and backups were encrypted. We knew the computers were password protected and screen locked. We knew essential items like the server and network equipment were physically caged and locked. Fortunately, they knocked over a bookcase and blocked their entry, so it wasn't a big deal. There's no accounting for idiocy.

Years later, I ran into the dentist who went through that original data breach at a dental school alumni event. She hugged me and told her colleagues how I saved her practice from becoming another statistic and how we kept all the patients. I don't think either of us are huggers, but her endless gratitude is humbling.

I consider this experience a best, worst-case scenario. It could have been horrible; the doctor could have lost everything so close to retirement. Or, I could have botched it and contributed to the worst-case scenario. We both learned a tremendous amount, and we both came out stronger in the end.

A JOURNEY INTO MULTIPLE BUSINESSES

As more calls came in for Data Breach consulting, I built a library of stories and examples to include in my courses. As more classes and lectures happened, more demand materialized. I'm thrilled to say that I have had ZERO clients on our proactive HIPAA program experience a data breach. Of the data breaches I've consulted on, ZERO received a fine or penalty from the state or federal government, no patient lawsuit, none have filed for bankruptcy or closed their practices. I don't claim to be magical; I just know that jumping into action and knowing the correct process makes a big difference in the outcome.

I don't sell HIPAA, or compliance, or even IT. I sell peace of mind. When the proverbial s*** hits the fan, you will have multiple layers in place to manage a predictable failure with a confined perimeter for how bad the situation will be. It will be a minor inconvenience instead of a major catastrophe. That peace of mind is what drives me to be better for everyone in my life - clients and family alike.

With all the extra demand on HIPAA, the IT division of ACS Technologies, LLC coasted, and I started neglecting it. In late 2019, I began toying with the idea of separating the divisions into different companies. Then COVID-19 hit, and the world came to a screeching halt. When things started getting back to this messed-up new normal, we resumed this transition.

Copper Penny Consulting, LLC was created to address speaking, coaching, consulting, education, and data breaches in January 2021. Since then, I've expanded our education offerings, adding California Dental Practice Act and enlarged the HIPAA program. We still work cooperatively with ACS and find that the clients who employ both companies are the most secure and easiest to manage. However, they are two separate entities with separate clients. As if this wasn't enough, I have even branched out into overseeing third-party vendors that integrate programs into dental practices and IT providers across the country.

I'd love to tell you that running multiple businesses with employees in both is fantastic, but the reality is there is double the work to do between them. I suppose the CEO in me is constantly seeing new opportunities, and I find it hard not to act on those. Things still change on the IT side that require my attention and currently we need another technician and someone to take over sales for me.

Copper Penny is demanding more and more of my time. My family needs me to be present in these formative years of my daughters' lives. My husband is a rock that I never expected in life; I always anticipated going at things alone. Don't get me wrong, we argue about the stupidest things - usually about him leaving the dishwasher open and me running into it (that's a story for another time). His endless patience and encouragement for me to reach toward dreams I didn't know I had and chase every opportunity is the reason you're reading this right now.

What's Next?

As I find myself in yet another professional transition period, I've recently reflected on the last 25 years working in healthcare. How I've gotten here, where I want to go, and all the obstacles along the way – yup, that teenager in me is still looking for projects to lead. Working in the primarily male-dominated industry of IT and security, I've found myself guarding what I say, lest anyone use a conversation to undercut or sabotage us.

As I've transitioned to speaking and consulting on HIPAA, Data Breaches, and the California Dental Practice Act the types of people and businesses I work with don't appear to be cutthroat like in the IT and business space. Many of my peers behave as peers, and I see a lot of "coopetition," cooperative competition. This environment is the type of business I've spent years hoping to find.

For too long, people labeled me as pushy, bitchy, and bossy. I've gotten a reputation for being thorough but a hard ass. Today, I am looking forward to this next chapter, where I am simply......the boss.

AMY WOOD

As CEO of Copper Penny Consulting, LLC and President of ACS Technologies, LLC, Amy Wood consults with businesses to address their Risk Management and HIPAA Compliance programs, both before and after a data breach. She helps implement proactive compliance programs into existing workflows and minimize the damage after a data breach.

Amy has worked in healthcare for more than 20 years. Her passion for risk management began after her own identity was compromised as a result of X-rays being lost from staff errors. That passion has turned into a commitment to provide an easy-to-understand approach to complex regulations. She maintains multiple industry certifications, including HCISPP, and maintains memberships with HHS 405(d), FBI Infragard, Healthcare Compliance Association, Academy of Dental Management Consultants, Speaking Consulting Network and American Academy of Dental Office Managers.

As a Continuing Education Provider through Academy of General Dentistry and Dental Board of California, Amy educates private practice and clinics individually, as well as dental associations, study clubs, disability groups, and other assemblies.

Her ability to relate to others and make things easy to understand is only one of the reasons North Bay Business Journal named her one of their "40 under 40's Ones to Watch." Amy and her husband are raising their three "bossy" daughters in Santa Rosa, CA.

To learn more about the People, Process, Technology approach to HIPAA or take one of Amy's courses, visit www.copperpennyconsulting.com. If you are in need of high-quality IT and security and are in northern California, visit us at www.acsdt.com.

CHAPTER 4

SPEAKING FROM EXPERIENCE: FINDING MY VOICE

Dr. Laila Hihaw

*"If there's one thing I've learned in life,
it's the power of using your voice."*
—Michelle Obama

When I turned 40, I didn't throw a party: I had an extravaganza with belly dancers, delicious Persian food and a DJ that got everyone on the dance floor. What I didn't know as I danced to Justin Timberlake's *Rock Your Body* was that everything was about to change, and it would take me almost a decade to discover who I am and what I want in life.

But that night, I was at the top of my game, and I was celebrating everything I'd built with friends and family.

I drew strength from every person who took the time to acknowledge my success as a mom and a dentist.

I love being a pediatric dentist. I'd built three successful practices that were booked solid at least six months in advance. My calendar ruled my days as I dashed between offices, coaxed children to sit still while I counted their teeth and explained treatments to anxious parents. At home, I had a loving husband, three small children and an indispensable nanny who filled the domestic gaps needed to keep our family and home running smoothly.

As the product of an African-American, single-parent home, I was taught security and financial stability came from working harder and sacrificing more than anyone else. No one could ever find out how I felt inside. Exhausted. Ill-equipped. I didn't know it at the time, but that fear of not being good enough is called imposter syndrome. It's a constant companion for so many women leaders in dentistry and medicine. We cope with it by trying to sustain the unsustainable and by giving 110% to everyone and everything we think is entitled to a piece of us.

Within days of my party, I was diagnosed with breast cancer. My brain couldn't process it, and I convinced myself it wasn't "real" cancer. My oncologist assured me it was.

Getting sick was the catalyst that ultimately led me to reevaluate my life. It took years to unpack all sorts of deeply held beliefs that I thought defined me. I measured success by the fullness of my schedule and the size of my dental practice. It took a lot of silent reflection and prayer before I could hear what was in my heart.

But I'm getting ahead of myself here. The truth is, I saw my illness and subsequent double mastectomy as yet another thing that had to be managed. I just needed to push through it as fast as I could so it wouldn't disrupt the lives of all the people who relied on me.

My doctor told me to take six to eight weeks off of work to recover, but I knew better. I was back managing my full workload in less than four. My first day sticks out in my mind. My husband, Alex, had to help me get dressed, and I remember asking my assistant to position the overhead light because I couldn't lift my arms over my head. I was pushing through, and, in my mind, I was doing the right thing. I think, as women, we're taught early on to put other people first at our own expense. I was merely following my programming.

When it was time to get reconstructive surgery with new implants, I felt nothing but relief. Not because they would make me whole again, but because I could finally have some time to rest. My thinking was so unhealthy that surgery seemed preferable to doing the work I loved. I now believe that my body was screaming for permission to slow down and take the time to recover. But I couldn't hear it, and no one else around me said the words "go home and get better."

Looking back now, I can see I was consumed with fear. If I didn't keep giving my all, everything would crumble, and the people around me would find out I wasn't superwoman. My business partner would have to cover for me. Our team, who depended on me for their livelihoods, wouldn't have the hours they needed to support their families. They'd also have to reschedule appointments and cope with disgruntled parents whose carefully scheduled lives my illness had interrupted.

My thinking was deeply flawed. Taking time off to recover wouldn't have destroyed the business, but the burden of responsibility and growing exhaustion I was feeling would most certainly have destroyed me. I felt overwhelmed, let down and completely worn out. Instead of being the bubbly, positive and supportive person everyone was used to, I was irritable and short-tempered. My sense of control was slipping away, and the more I checked out of my practice responsibilities, the more I lost the respect of my team. I prayed that my husband, an academic physician, would be offered an out-of-state job. It was the only way out that would allow me to give up everything without the shame of feeling like a failure.

My state of mind was taking a toll on all those around me. My business partner and leadership team staged an intervention. We'd reached the point where we were at risk of losing key staff. They suggested I find a therapist or life coach to help me get back to my old self.

I'd never even heard of a life coach but fate intervened. I met Leslie Fuqua Williams, Life & Leadership Coach, in my gynecologist's waiting room. She showed me how to step back and take a long hard look at my life, what I wanted and where I was going. What I saw, I didn't like. Could I really have been living a narrative that wasn't even mine for 40 years?

For as long as I can remember, my mother wanted me to become a doctor. She reasoned that people are always getting sick, so being a doctor would guarantee the financial stability that she never had as a single parent on a teacher's salary. She taught me that, as a woman of color, I'd have to work twice as hard as everyone else. It was advice that had served me well. I'd achieved so much, but I also saw that it was time for me to write my own script.

I took a deeper look at my practice, too. Keeping everyone around me happy wasn't the way to my happiness. I was more than a dentist, a mom and a wife. With guidance from my new life coach, reflection and prayer, I started to understand I'd smothered and silenced my inner voice. Then I promptly lost my ability to speak. My voice, it would seem, was beginning to fight back.

With Coach Leslie's help, I was able to open my mind to new ideas and look forward to it. She led me through her *What's NEXT?*™ framework designed to help women get unstuck on their journey.

N – What's NOT Happening?

E – What do I EXPECT?

X – What would be EXTRAORDINARY?

T – What's the TIMELY opportunity?

It took years to answer these questions and reinvent myself. Finding my inner voice, listening to it and ultimately using it for the things that matter to me was genuinely revolutionary, even if it was a path with twists and turns.

Writing my book was one of those wrong turns. I'd always dreamed of being an author. I wanted to share what I'd learned during my transformation with other high achievers who were driving towards goals without understanding why those goals were important. So, I found a self-publishing coach. He persuaded me to write about what I knew best and find a topic to build my authority as a pediatric dentist. He promised this would be easier, faster and more effective than my original plan.

Writing any book is challenging, but writing one when your heart isn't in it is excruciating. It took every ounce of discipline I had to complete it. *Cavity Free Kids: How to Care for Your Kids' Teeth from Birth Through Their Teenage Years* cost me energy, time and a lot of money to bring it and an accompanying website, TheMommyDentist.com, to life.

It was published in 2020, and reached the Amazon bestseller list. I'm very proud of it, but I'm sorry I didn't have the strength to listen to my inner voice. Despite the book's success, it wasn't the right passion project at that point in my life. However, it taught me how vital it is to listen to myself, rather than those around me. It's true, we hold the answers within us.

It is worth remembering that we are multidimensional beings. We are so much more than how we earn our living. When I studied what made me feel good, I noticed the impact motivational, keynote and expert speakers had on me. I wondered if sharing everything I'd experienced could do the same for other people.

In 2017, I finally felt brave enough to submit an idea to the American Academy of Pediatric Dentistry. I gave a presentation titled *Dentistry Doesn't Do It for Me Anymore— How to Get Your Spark Back* the following year at the annual meeting in Hawaii. It felt liberating and exciting, and it gave me the courage to speak up. I was finally learning how to use my voice, and people were interested in what I had to say.

Sharing your gifts with other people matters because they aren't for you alone: They belong to the community of people you can help and influence. As dentists and healthcare providers, we are teachers and role models within our practices and communities. Whatever way you decide is right for you, using your voice can bring about powerful change in ways that you least expect.

Not long ago, I came across an alarming statistic in the New Dentist News from the American Dental Association: Only 3.8% of all dentists in the U.S. are Black, only 5.2% are Hispanic, and a mere 1.1% are American Indians, Alaska Natives or Pacific Islanders.

Has nothing changed in the 20 years since I earned my dental degree? Was there anything I could do about it? I did what any modern woman would do, I turned to social media. I shared the statistic on my personal Facebook page and wrote, "So here's the situation. Whose kid can I mentor?"

My Facebook blew up. Parents and grandparents were reaching out for help. What started as a single post has since grown into the national nonprofit, Diversity in Dentistry Mentorships, Inc. The organization aims to provide students from historically underrepresented groups with the mentoring they need to get into this profession. Since 2018, we have grown our community to include over 1,400 dentists, pre-dental students, dental educators, parents and caregivers to educate and empower students to explore the rewarding career of dentistry. By using my voice, I found my passion and am on a mission to diversify and nurture the next generation of leaders in dentistry.

Finding your passion, living your joy, listening to your voice and using it to make the world a better place is not just noble, it is the best way I know to honor who you are and what you can contribute to the world. Finding your purpose brings clarity and a sense that you are doing what you were put on this earth to do. When you're faced with an important decision, it empowers you to make the right choice for the right reasons.

I found my voice and have used it to build my authority. I've channeled it into writing, speaking and leading my nonprofit organization. I'm so grateful to everyone who walked this path with me and supported me on this journey to self-awareness.

I encourage you to find your unique voice too. Your path will be different from mine, but whether self-expression means creating art, starting a podcast or advocating for equity and inclusion, the most important thing you can do is be true to yourself and write the narrative for the life you want to lead.

As innovative women in medicine, you are making a positive impact on the lives of others in the communities you serve. You are working in your gifts and are grateful for all the blessings your work brings you. I felt the same way, but my spirit was telling me there was more I was meant to do. My heart's desire is to empower high-achieving, compassionate women like you, to quiet the busyness of your life and seek your unique voice. Only then will you find the power to create change, transform lives, build your authority, and ultimately find joy!

If you want to amplify your voice by becoming a speaker, author or nonprofit founder, I am here to help you become the leader in your field. I have created a course that will take you through the steps I took to regain my voice and reinvent myself while continuing to practice as a pediatric dentist. This transformational course will help you discover your unique voice and how to transform your life while impacting the lives of others. Join the waitlist to be the first to know when the course is open on my website https://drlailahishaw.com and let's continue to speak from experience together.

DR. LAILA HISHAW

Dr. Laila Hishaw is an entrepreneurial thought leader and authority in children's oral health. She is a board-certified pediatric dentist and Fellow of the American Academy of Pediatric Dentistry, a distinction held by only 3% of pediatric dentists.

Hishaw is an owner of Tucson Smiles Pediatric Dentistry and was featured on Discovery Health Channel for her role in diagnosing a rare disorder in a patient. Her book, *Cavity Free Kids: How to Care for Your Kids' Teeth from Birth Through Their Teenage Years,* is an Amazon bestseller, and she is a national speaker on pediatric dentistry, diversity, and topics relevant to women in healthcare. She has been published in Thrive Global and the ADA News.

In 2018, Hishaw founded the national nonprofit organization, Diversity in Dentistry Mentorships Inc., to encourage Black and other students from underrepresented groups to consider careers in dentistry. The organization has been featured in Yahoo! Finance, Black Enterprise and the

ADA News. In 2020-2021 she was selected for the American Dental Association Institute for Diversity in Leadership.

As a wife, mother of three, entrepreneur, and philanthropist, she is passionate about sharing tools and her experiences to aid her colleagues and emerging leaders in dentistry towards success in every aspect of their lives. She lives in Tucson, Arizona with her family and her rescue pets, Stormie and Miles.

Diversity in Dentistry Mentorships, Inc.

Sign up to become a mentor:

https://diversitydentistry.org

Contribute:

https://www.paypal.com/paypalme/ diversityindentistry

Need a Speaker for Your Event?

Hire me to speak: https://drlailahishaw.com

Get My Book and Download Free Resources

Cavity Free Kids: How to Care for Your Kids' Teeth from Birth Through Their Teenage Years

by Laila B Hishaw, DDS

https://themommydentist.com

CHAPTER 5

LIVING AN EXTRAORDINARY LIFE WITH PURPOSE

Dr. Hoa Nguyen

Escaping Vietnam for the American Dream

I'd like to first share a bit of my family's story. The Fall of Saigon in Vietnam was April 30, 1975. My family was from South Vietnam and fled the country later in 1978, leaving everything behind in hopes of a better life in a new country. My dad had a boat and helped lots of people escape to Manila, Philippines, knowing that everyone was risking their lives in hopes of a better opportunity in an unknown place. Imagine a wooden boat in the middle of the night, jam-packed with scared families going out to the open sea with little food or water.

The rough waters at sea almost killed everyone, but thankfully my family and the others made it to Manila and stayed in the refugee camps. That was where I was born. My parents had my two older brothers with them on the boat. They always wanted to come to America for us to have the opportunity to live the American dream.

We came to the United States when I was eight years old, and our family of five all lived in one bedroom of a house that we shared with others. We moved to several other places before settling in New Orleans in a small trailer my parents bought for $3,000.

I was only 12 years old the days I had a gun put to my head in the projects of New Orleans. Needless to say, I've built some tough skin growing up seeing all sorts of things. My parents worked so hard, and my mom would cry in silence sometimes hoping we wouldn't notice because we were not living the American dream the way she and my dad had hoped for. Finances were always a struggle, and both of my parents always worked seven days a week to make ends meet.

I vividly remember the morning I was getting ready to go to school, and I sat down next to my dad who happened to sleep on the sofa that night. One of his hands was still resting behind his head and the other hand was resting on his stomach. I sat quietly before heading to school so I wouldn't wake him up. My dad was always so selfless and always helped anyone he could, regardless of what financial position we were in. He would take homeless people home, feed them, and do anything he could to get them on their feet again. Needless to say, his empathy and love for helping others really inspired us.

I thought it was rather unusual when my friend's mom came to my school later that day to check on me. That was when I found out that my dad had already passed away in his sleep when I was sitting next to him that morning. I was 13 at that time, and I was devastated.

My mom now had to carry the full weight of the family, and she continued to work seven days a week, 14–16-hour workdays, and do the best she could to take care of us. I started working at the age of 10 in our small family business, so my days were school and then straight to work to help my mom. None of us had weekend breaks, holiday breaks, or any type of summer vacations. I continued that with my mom until I went to optometry school.

My family has endured so many challenges beyond just financial hardships, but we always had each other, which was the biggest blessing. My mom has always been and will always be my rock of strength, compassion, and love. She worked hard all her life and always carried a smile on her face. You'd never see the deep, heavy pain she was carrying in her heart from the outside, but we knew her resilience was for us.

My brother and I wanted to do our best to show our parents that their sacrifices would not be in vain and that we would maximize any and all resources to create our own opportunities. I tried my best in academia, became Valedictorian, and went on to receive a scholarship to Tulane University, the top private university in New Orleans. There, I continued to get my doctorate in optometry. My brother joined the Navy and finished a residency in family medicine and then a secondary residency in aerospace medicine. He then became Lieutenant Commander in the Navy. Freedom and the ability to achieve anything you believe is priceless. We are living the American dream and paying it forward to help others do the same.

Finding the Love of My Life

I was always very shy, introverted, timid, and a loner. At a very young age, I was laser-focused on doing well in order to take care of my mom and help her to retire. English was my third language, and when we came to the U.S., I went through many schools because my family was moving so much, looking for work. I was teased a lot, and I kept to myself with the exception of a few close friends. I never felt like I fit in. I always felt unfulfilled and like I was not good enough.

I didn't realize that my life was about to change when I met this young fellow named Jaime Gonzalez in optometry school. He was my lab partner in the clinic, and we had to perform eye injections on each other. He wasn't like anyone I had ever met before. I had built so many layers of protection around my heart, and he was the first one who was able to pierce through. We both came from very humble backgrounds, but he was full of life, sociable, tall, handsome, and I just loved the way I felt around him. He brought out the best in me and made me believe in myself. He was a visionary with huge dreams. We started dating, and I knew very early in our relationship that he was my soulmate and lover for life.

In the Face of Death

I was doing my last year's clinical rotation in Austin, TX while Jaime was doing his clinical rotations in Dallas, TX, when I was driving back from visiting him over the weekend. Suddenly, one of the big tires stacked on top of the truck in front of me came flying down towards me. I saw my life flash in front of me. I quickly swerved to the left where there was a ditch. I lost control and my car flipped multiple times before turning upside down into that ditch. People immediately came over to pull me out of the broken window, and it was truly a miracle that I survived with only minor injuries. Jaime was my knight in shining armor who came to take care of me. That moment of getting a second chance changed my perspective on life forever. I really started to appreciate life more, and I was truly grateful to be alive.

After being with my husband for nine years, we were finally blessed with our little baby girl, Athena Lily

Gonzalez. Having our daughter was not an easy journey and it changed our priorities. After having her, we wanted to spend more time with her than our current way of living would allow. The moment she came into our lives, she made such a positive impact in our hearts.

Our nanny, Maria, started with us when Athena was six weeks old. When Athena was almost four, we received a phone call from our nanny's husband that Maria was just rushed to the hospital. When we got to the hospital, the doctor told us she had stage four metastatic breast cancer and she would only have a short time to live, with no treatment options since it had already spread everywhere in her body.

When we came into Maria's room after receiving the news, we couldn't control our tears. She smiled and hugged us so hard. She told us not to cry and that she was so grateful that her two beautiful daughters survived against all odds. Her twin girls were only a little over a year old, and they were preemies with so many complications and surgeries. She said it was time for her to be with God soon, and that she was so grateful for every day that she was still alive to be with her family. She was always happy, grateful, compassionate, and so kind.

She passed away a few weeks after that hospital visit. Her memory will forever have a huge impact on our lives as she was so grateful, even in the face of death.

Becoming Entrepreneurs

When Jaime and I graduated from optometry school, we had over $300,000 in combined student loan debt. We were both fortunate enough to find full-time work at a private practice in Dallas Fort Worth immediately after graduation. We will always remember celebrating that very first paycheck, because we could finally retire our parents who had always worked so hard. We continued to live in a small one-bedroom apartment so we could help take care of our parents. We were so happy that we could do that now.

We picked up extra relief work to make additional money and would frequently work seven days a week for 21 days straight before taking a one-day break. We never had much time to travel or take breaks because we were so focused on saving enough money to buy our own practice.

We always dreamed of having our own practice and being our own bosses.

After four and a half years of working for someone else, we were able to open our own practice in Dallas, named Eye Pieces. We worked six days a week at our practice and still worked additional days, and we purchased our second practice three years later. Our main focus has always been meaningful relationships in business and in our personal lives. We have successfully grown both of our practices and have maintained very loyal staff and patients that continue to see us after 15 years of practice. Building trust and maintaining consistent integrity has always been the foundation of everything we do.

Trading Time for Money

One of our passions is traveling the world, immersing ourselves in different cultures, and being able to give back in a meaningful way financially or with our time through volunteering. After Athena was born, we really wanted to make sure we could spend quality family time together and be involved as much as we could with all of her milestones.

We wanted to find other avenues to achieve financial freedom and time. We didn't want to continue trading time for money without other avenues of passive income. We wanted diversification, and we knew real estate was the vehicle through which most people achieved wealth. We wanted to be able to build a legacy business for our daughter and truly have the flexibility to live life by our design. That's when our real estate journey began.

We started out by passively investing with others and leveraging their teams and experience. We then loved it so much that we leveraged other partners to actively syndicate deals ourselves. The more we learned and grew, the more we realized what we didn't know. For years, as doctors, we were trained to take care of patients, but we were not taught financial literacy and all the benefits of other avenues of investing, besides the typical 401k and IRAs.

We've now been able to transition almost fully into real estate, and we now practice twice a month because we want to and not because we have to. We have built a great work culture with a loyal team and great associate doctors, and have implemented systems so we don't need to physically be at our practices for them to continue to grow. We are able to have diversified cash flow from our real estate portfolio and our two practices.

We've been able to travel with our daughter all over the world and have been able to do mission trips in other countries. We're able to help transform communities, give residents safe, affordable places to live, and help other families leverage our team and invest with us to provide passive income for them. We want to help others achieve more financial freedom and time freedom.

The outcome that we receive from being involved in real estate is my passion. The impact we get to make truly fulfills us. Life balance is so important to us. Our life balance checkpoints are faith, family, fun, focus, and fulfillment. One of the quotes that sticks with me is, "Don't get so busy making a living, you forget to make a life."

Empowering Others to Dream Big

It took many years of peeling all the layers of the onion to find myself and find my power within. Jaime and I have always enjoyed mentoring youth, and seeing them succeed gives us so much joy. Knowing that we had an impact on their journey allows us to dream bigger and makes us want to help even more people. Multifamily real estate investing is yet one other vehicle to carry out our mission to help empower other families to live life by their own design.

We teach others how to diversify their income and add a stream of passive income investing in stabilized, cash-flowing apartment communities. It's a great way to be involved in real estate without having to be a landlord, yet receive all the benefits of multifamily leveraging an experienced team with a track record. Some of the benefits of multifamily real estate investing include cash flow, more conservative asset class, appreciation of the asset, accelerated depreciation leading to substantial tax advantages, increased scalability to grow your portfolio, building equity and making a positive impact transforming these apartment communities. We partner with other non-profit organizations to give back to the residents and make the apartment communities a safe, clean place that residents are proud to call their home. Building meaningful relationships and trust with our teams, investors, residents, and patients is extremely important to us.

I also personally want to empower other young women like myself and give them hope and inspiration that all the strength they need is right within themselves already. While I'm still here, I want to be that voice for others, showing them how to speak up, know they are good enough, take massive action, live with purpose, and make a difference in this world.

Don't be afraid to dream big! Someone once told me, if your dream doesn't scare you, it's not big enough.

DR. HOA NGUYEN

Hoa Nguyen loves to help others grow and to educate investors about passive income opportunities through apartment investing She is an entrepreneur, business leader, eye doctor, and an accredited real estate investor and syndicator. She has ownership in over $170M in real estate acquisitions and invested in over 4,600 units. She owns successful multi-million-dollar eyecare practices and co-founded 20/20 Platinum Capital to help families invest passively in multifamily real estate. Email her for a complimentary due diligence checklist on passive investing and to book a free 15-minute consultation at hoa@eyepiecesinvesting.com or www.2020investorgroup.com. She is available to speak and would love to spread hope to others.

Tweetable: Believing in your own power with conviction is the foundation of progress. You make a difference if you make that your focus. Life is too short to play small.

CHAPTER 6

BULDING RELATIONSHIPS FOR SUCCESS

Dr. Vi Ho

I am an endodontist living in Cypress, Texas and have been in practice for about ten years. It is an honor to share my story with you.

I was born and raised in a multigenerational family in Phan Rang, Vietnam that included grandmother, aunts, uncles and cousins. Our living conditions were tight physically and financially. In 1992, my immediate family (myself and my mom, dad, and little sister) was blessed with an opportunity to immigrate to America because we had adopted an Amerasian brother.

As a part of the transition before landing on the American soil, we were placed in a refugee camp in Bataan, Philippines for six months. There, we were given the opportunity to learn the new English language. As with many refugee camps, it was deficient in basic supplies such as water, electricity and food. It was the first time in my life that I came to the realization that I needed to figure out something to help my family in any way that I could. My contributions during our time at the refugee camp were earning extra money with a fruit stand of my own, collecting enough water on a daily basis for my family's use, washing clothes, cleaning dishes and taking care of my little sister. My tasks then may seem too much for an eight-year-old but I did not feel the weight of them. Instead, I got to experience the gratification of contribution and a sense of self-worth.

After the Philippines, we landed in Alexandria, Louisiana. My American dream before we arrived was very simple: I dreamt of arriving at a home with a refrigerator full of red apples waiting for me. My dream did not come true. Instead, we were met with poor living conditions and deficiencies not so different from the refugee camp.

Very soon after, we moved to Baton Rouge, Louisiana in search for better opportunities, a better life. Our life did get better. It was better because my parents had jobs, opportunities to earn money. They both worked 12 hours a day, six to seven days a week with jobs such as nail technician, mechanic and crawfish and crab peelers and processors. My parents had the weight of earning to care for their immediate family and extended families back in Vietnam.

With such a rigorous work schedule, they were gone from home a lot. Again, I knew I had to step in and contribute. I took care of my sister and the little brother who came along a few years later. At the age of nine, besides all of the house chores and babysitting, I started to cook for my family. After a few meals, I became very passionate with cooking. Cooking for my family made me feel proud and satisfied. I felt proud because I could provide healthy meals to my parents after long work hours. I was very aware that healthy homecooked meals were crucial to our wellness. I was satisfied because it allowed me to be creative. Most importantly, for a young girl, it gave me confidence. The confidence that I had a skill that could carry me through life if all else failed.

I grew up in a very atypical Asian family in the sense of education. My parents never once demanded academic success or career goals for us. Instead, we were always encouraged to eat well and sleep well because health is wealth. It was like a chant throughout my growing years under their roof. The only true demand was for us to make them proud by being good citizens. So, as you can imagine, I never had the pressure of meeting expectations and was very comfortable with being average. Peer pressure was never an issue. I had a lot of time to get to know myself and what it was that I really wanted in life. Of course, at the time, my parents were not aware that they were doing me a great service that later shaped and helped me through life.

At the age of 15, in my junior year of high school, we visited Houston, Texas. I decided I needed to leave the slow-growing state of Louisiana to move to that bigger city. I felt deep down inside that I needed to be in this new city to prosper, to help my family out of financial stress and for a better future. So, I told my parents by the end of Junior year I would be moving. They were shocked to say the least. It was mostly because of my determination. My mom was supportive but it was hard for my dad. Mom finally convinced dad under one condition: If I did not turn out good, it would be all mom's fault.

I lived with my aunt's family in Houston in a small run-down two-bedroom apartment. I shared a room with three younger male cousins. It was just a place to sleep at night. I was going through my senior year of high school in the new city. When school end at 3:30 every day, I went straight to work as a dental assistant, working until late at night. Ending the job at eight or nine in the evening was normal. Working to 12 midnight was not uncommon either. Those working hours may be an issue for other people but for me, it was great. I had an opportunity to earn money! I needed to earn to take care of myself and support my parents in any way that I could. I gave myself a dollar a day to spend.

When I was done with high school, I was able to give my mom a few thousand dollars before I went off to college. Being able to contribute and take care of my family gave me peace of mind when I was no longer at home to help out.

I moved on to the well-respected Texas A&M university with a full scholarship. I honestly did not feel like I was truly deserving of this blessing. I felt that way because although I had a high grade point average, it was from the most bottom tier high school in the city. I never took any advanced college classes in high school like most other students at the university. I did not have any distinctions. What did the university see in me?

Because of my ill-preparation for college, I struggled my first semester. I was a grade level above failing although I felt like I studied so hard. I was terrified to see how my classmates in Chemistry class understood everything that was like a foreign language to me. I felt so far behind that I thought I could never catch up. I was not smart enough for college. I never even dreamed for college anyways. I was right, college is only for smart people. I asked my mom to let me quit. I cried to her and said I wanted to go home. It was painful to be met with failure.

Once I got done with the crying and the thought of giving up, I collected myself. I said to myself, "I can not a be quitter." I re-focused my mindset. Instead of studying hard to earn that high grade or reach for that distinction, I told myself to study so that I could learn something new. I learned that the letter grades of B or C or D do not matter too much:

What mattered was going back to look at the questions that I got wrong and learn from them. When doing so, I felt really proud of myself because I was not scared to go back and look at my "failures." When I went back and faced them, I learned how to make them right and not to make those mistakes again. The knowledge that I gained from facing my failure was solid and would stick with me for life.

This experience was life-changing for me. I never looked at challenges the same way anymore. Fear no longer entered into the picture to affect or prevent my goals. Instead, I just shoot for my goal with honesty, integrity and bravery. When you take fear of failure out of the equation, you become brave. With this approach, even if you fail to reach that specific goal, you never really fail completely because you have learned and gained knowledge or experience that could enhance other aspects or goals in your life.

With that new mindset, my grades improved tremendously. Learning became fun. I went on into dental school, which was like a dream come true. How could a small-town girl from lower-class, minimally-educated parents get an opportunity to become a dentist! To be called a doctor! I said I could not ask for or become anything more. I was wrong! I graduated dental school with honors, being in the top three of my class and was immediately accepted to a class of two residents in endodontic specialty training. After that, I went on to open my own practice and made it successful.

Of course, I was faced with fear and worries when I decided to become a business owner, but the same principles and experiences I learned in college got me through.

The whole journey from high school to becoming a dental specialist has been life-changing for me. Not in the sense of the obtaining a specialist title or financial rewards, in the sense of my perspective and outlook in life. It has made my life a lot simpler and more enjoyable. It gave me confidence and strength to get through the toughest of times with the right mindset.

Throughout this journey, I also learned relationship-building is so important. You cannot go through life and make it successful alone. I love the quote "if you want to go fast, you go alone, if you want to go far, you go together." I'm gifted with a cooking skill and the love of nurturing others. Cooking for others is how I show people I care and form relationships. As I see it, people have differences, but one thing most people have in common is the love for good food. A good meal brings people together.

I have a decent-sized family with three children and both of my parents. Raising my children with healthy body and mind is important to me, and spending quality family time is always my number one goal. I use cooking as the channel to achieve this. I teach my children how to cook and have everyone involved in meal preparation. I try to give them opportunities to experience the joy and satisfaction of contribution and collaboration. In this process, I'm also able to bring awareness of being health conscious. At the end of the day, as a mother, I want to keep my children as healthy as possible and that starts with healthy habits and customs.

I care as much for my patients as my family. I always search for ways to provide the best care in the most natural way possible. My endodontic practice is taking an integrative approach to care. This includes the use of laser, ozone therapies, platelet rich fibrin and nutritional counseling. There is nothing better than supporting the body to heal on its own. Whole-body health should always be considered. I believe true happiness arrives when your methods of professional practice are in alignment with the way you live your life.

I view my own success as how much positive impact I have made and how much I have served. With that in mind, I created a cooking community to share tips and lessons to eat and cook healthier and I also created a dental study club to bring colleagues together to share knowledge to improve quality of care. I invite you all to join my Facebook groups, "The Ultimate Relationship Chef" or "The Cypress Endodontics Study Club."

DR. VI HO

Dr. Vi Ho was born in Vietnam and grew up in Baton Rouge, Louisiana. She received her Bachelor's Degree in Biology from Texas A&M University. Immediately upon graduation, she entered Creighton University School of Dentistry and graduated in the top 2% of her class. While at Creighton University School of Dentistry, she was selected as a member of the national dental honor society, Omicron Kappa Upsilon. The membership was limited to those dental students who have distinguished themselves by excellence in scholarship, while demonstrating exemplary traits of character and potential qualities for future professional growth and attainments. Dr. Ho was then accepted to a class size of two residents at the University of Texas School of Dentistry - Houston to receive three extra years of endodontic specialty training and a Master's Degree in Science of Dentistry. During her time as an endodontic resident, she was involved in her own research of root canal irrigation and served as a teaching assistant to dental students.

After years of practicing endodontics, Dr. Ho decided to establish her own practice, Cypress Endodontics. Dr. Ho's philosophy is that a patient cannot see what you're doing but they can feel what you're doing and how you're doing it. For every patient, she strives to hear from them at the end of the procedure that they felt comfortable and confident with her care. To her, that's the professional satisfaction and pride that she always aims for. Dr. Ho's other loves aside from endodontics are cooking and being a homeschooling mom to her three children ages 8, 7 and 4.

CHAPTER 7

GRIT, GRIN, AND STILETTOS: LESSONS IN LEADERSHIP AND RESILIENCE

Dr. Jonelle Grant Anamelechi

"Do not judge me by my successes, judge me by how many times I fell down and got back up again."
–Nelson Mandela

Resilience. What exactly is it? Where does it come from? And why do leaders need it? According to the Merriam Webster online dictionary, resilience is "an ability to recover from or adjust easily to misfortune or change." That is a good definition. I doubt there's a person who hasn't looked misfortune in the eye and wanted to rewrite their story. What has this got to do with leadership? From my perspective, everything.

Leaders are people who step up when others won't or can't. They take risks, do what needs doing and show others the way even if they aren't sure of the path ahead, and every step looks scary. It is about getting back up even when you've been knocked down so hard you can't stop shaking.

With the right mindset, I believe you can turn devastating situations into opportunities for personal or professional growth. Keeping an open mind makes your heart receptive to new ideas and innovative solutions.

I'm a daughter, wife, mom and pediatric dentist. I own two practices in Washington, DC and Maryland, and I lead a team of 17 amazing women. I've been a professor at Children's National Hospital since 2013, and I'm an adjunct faculty member at MedStar Georgetown University Hospital with the Department of Pediatrics and the School of Law and Equity.

People tell me that I make success look easy, but looks can be deceiving. My journey's ups have been tremendous. Some of the downs have been truly crushing. I've picked myself up out of the dirt and found the inner strength to keep reaching for my dreams more times than I can count.

I've been cast in the fires of resilience. I want to share some of the lessons I've learned with other women in the hope that it helps them overcome some of the things that might stop us from achieving our potential.

I grew up on a family farm in South Carolina to parents who wanted the best for their children. It was a childhood rich in love and support even though we weren't materially well off. My family may call it "stubbornness" but I prefer to think of it as the resourcefulness I learned watching my parents deal with whatever difficulty their day held without complaint.

As I face the daily challenges of raising my children, I often look back and marvel at my parents' wisdom. By setting a good example, they gave me the tools to survive marriage and motherhood - the ultimate test of my resilience. My parents said "no" to me frequently. I didn't know it then, but it was a gift.

"Can I play now?"

"No. Finish your homework."

"Can I give up piano lessons?"

"No. You need to learn not to quit."

Every "no" had a lesson. Taken together, they fostered my stamina to keep trying. Falling down was okay at our house; staying down wasn't.

I vividly remember when the career guidance teacher at my high school refused to write me a college reference. She was convinced I hadn't a hope of getting into Duke University to start my journey to become a dentist. I was mortified. The strength of her conviction stung, but it also made me more determined (especially after the good old Grant family pep talk) to write a better application and dig deeper to find a solution.

So, I swallowed my nerves and asked my own pediatric dentist if I could work at her office after school and then petitioned her to write the reference I needed. I got into Duke. I believe that success tasted sweeter because I had to drive harder. It set me up with the skills to look for unconventional ways to achieve my objectives.

Of course, taking responsibility for what you want isn't all pushing and fighting. Sometimes you have to give yourself permission to pause and regroup. During my pediatric dental residency at the University of North Carolina at

Chapel Hill, I ran into some challenges that meant I needed to step away from my studies.

The break gave me time to dust myself off and come up with a strategy. When the time was right, I restarted my residency because there are people out there that will give you a chance and allow you to prove yourself. I completed it in a year instead of two.

I discovered the incredible value of knowing when to stop and reevaluate - a critical leadership skill. Taking a break is not the same as giving up. Eating humble pie never feels good, but it can provide the time you need to work out what to do next to make your dream come true.

My dream was to open a pediatric dental practice and now I own two - one in the neighborhood I live in. Opening a dental office takes a significant investment - equipment, insurance, a lease, a staff and more. I was bursting with enthusiasm, jotted down some numbers on a pad and thought I had everything figured out. However, starting a business is a more complicated endeavor than that. To be taken seriously, you need to act like a businessperson. There was no way anyone was going to give me a half million dollars in funding without a well-prepared business plan.

I had to learn how to research my market, identify my audience, predict my running costs and create a plan to realize my goals. Acquiring these new skills took time and yet another hearty slice of that not-so-delicious humble pie.

However, I can honestly say I wouldn't be where I am today without doing this foundational work. Learning business skills has given me the confidence to lead my team, market my practice and use the business's financial statements to manage resources and keep us on a steady heading.

Understanding the business side of dentistry put me in the best possible position to survive when the pandemic took hold in early 2020. As dentists, we all had to get creative to keep our doors open, make sure employees and patients were safe and provide continuity of care to kids whose teeth kept on growing despite the world turning upside down. Our costs went up as our revenue went down. Businessman and Artist Jay-Z once said, "The genius thing that we did was, we didn't give up." We have recovered and even though we lost eighty percent of my team, we came through with more team grit and grins than ever before.

As a practice owner, it sometimes feels like there's an endless stream of challenges sent to test the limits of your resilience and courage. Team members have problems that you need to accommodate, equipment breakdowns cause chaos, reliable suppliers go bad overnight and personal emergencies can strike at the worst of times.

About three years after starting my practice, I sustained an injury while performing surgery. Rest assured, my patient was fine, but I wasn't. Within days, I was the one on the gurney getting prepped for the operating room. My illness sent tremors through my business. Even with well-defined processes in place to help key employees step up while I recovered, I was worried sick.

Being prepared for the unexpected is a primary leadership responsibility and an essential part of building resiliency in your practice. Every business needs a contingency plan for when things go wrong. The best ones are created in collaboration with your leadership team. Expecting your team to make the right choices and think through every eventuality during a crisis without a blueprint is neither realistic nor fair.

I believe that preparation is one of the best things you can do. Hiring a mentor or coach who has walked the path before is invaluable. They'll show you where pitfalls lurk and help you avoid them, and they'll give you the confidence you need to overcome your fears. A good one will point out opportunities you weren't aware of, solutions you hadn't considered and then help you choose the best options. They are there to guide you, not tell you what to do. You decide whether to take their advice and what you think will work best in your situation.

No one makes it through life without facing adversity. Whether those challenges take you down or lift you up depends on your grit, resilience and the ability to pick yourself up even on the darkest days. I know I'll continue to face new and unexpected challenges, and I hope I'll have the stamina to meet them head-on - likely while wearing my favorite pair of stilettos. My dreams are worth fighting for, and so are yours.

DR. JONELLE ANAMELECHI

Dr. Jonelle Anamelechi obtained her undergraduate degree from Duke University.

She started her path in dentistry at the University of North Carolina at Chapel Hill (UNC-CH) Adams School of Dentistry and completed her Masters of Public Health in Maternal and Child Health at the UNC-CH School of Global Health. Dr. Anamelechi attended St. Joseph Regional Medical Center for her pediatric dental residency program. She opened Children's Choice Pediatric Dentistry and Orthodontics in New Carrollton, MD and Washington, DC, and built the practice of her dreams entirely from scratch. She is attending faculty at Children's National Hospital in the Division of Oral Health, Medstar Georgetown Hospital in the Department of Pediatric Medicine, and Guest Faculty at Georgetown School of Law. Her national and international work has focused on children with craniofacial abnormalities, tethered tissues and their link to poor oral health, and health equity for children with special challenges.

Dr. Anamelechi is a speaker, clinician, author, and policy advocate. She been featured on ABC News, NBC News, and Dentaltown, a national dental magazine. As co-editor, she is launching a book titled "What Should Mommy Do for Their Child's Oral Health," to be released fall 2021.

Book Dr. Anamelechi as a speaker at your next event and join her Mom-Inspired, Dentist-Approved community at: www.mominspireddentistapproved.com

CHAPTER 8

THE BALANCE OF A MOMPRENEUR

Quyen Le

The Balance of a Mompreneur

At the age of 17, my family and I came to the U.S.A. We didn't speak any English, but being the only kid in the family who was still in school, I was determined to finish high school and then graduate college with a bachelor's degree in accounting. I did just that.

I landed a corporate accounting job at the same time I met my future husband, Nathan. He was still in dental school, and we were married about a year after Nathan's graduation. Although I had a good-paying corporate job, I wanted to take another step to become a certified public accountant.

I took additional night and weekend classes and sat for my CPA exam. Two weeks after our first son was born, I was notified that I had passed my exams and became a CPA. Nathan had already bought an established dental practice with his partner right after school and then started a second one. Before we hit our 30th birthdays, we were over 1/2 a million dollars in the debt with our personal mortgage, student loans, and business loans.

And, our family life got even busier with our newborn, Jaden.

I was a very strong, independent, self-driven person but becoming a new mom was more challenging than I thought. Since Nathan had two businesses to run, I was left in charge of my son's doctor appointments along with household finances, house maintenance, and chores. Then, when we had our second son, Lennon, I had to take more time off from work for his doctor appointments and care. So, a crazy idea came to mind: Why don't I open my CPA firm to have more time for my sons? I could create my own schedule and take off time when I needed to. So, I started my own business from scratch.

At the same time, my friend, Angie Dong, introduced me to the real estate market. We were driving in the rain looking for real estate deals, and I became excited about the additional financial opportunities that I saw. But, every time we seemed to have found an ideal house to invest in, my husband talked me out of it.

My husband had another friend who also was a real estate broker and had advised Nathan *not* to get into real estate. Why? Not only was the market overpriced, according to Nathan's friend, but he felt that real estate was not a good vehicle to build wealth. In 2008, most of his tenants had taken off without paying their rent and left his rental homes in shambles. He lost everything through foreclosures because he didn't have enough capital to bring these homes back to a livable condition. It took determination and effort (and by that, I mean consistent nagging) to finally convince Nathan to rent our old house out as a market test before investing in rental homes.

Becoming a business owner and being a mom of two small kids, a real estate investor, and being married to an entrepreneur didn't work in my favor! I had too much on my plate, and I didn't have any energy left for my kids and family. I knew there had to be a better way, but I eventually let go of my CPA business to focus on family and other priorities. And, even though we managed our financial challenges so well that we got out of debt in our 30's, deep down inside, letting go of my business somehow made me feel like a loser. I was afraid of judgment and inevitable questions ("Hey, Quyen, what happened to the business?"). It took me a long time to realize that to make room for something better I needed to take away things that didn't work well for my family and me. And I did.

HOWEVER, what I have discovered through my journey is that I did have a passion for real estate. By being a good landlord, I can provide low-income families the opportunity to live in better neighborhoods and attend better schools, hoping that the next generation will have a higher standard of living than their parents. That is still the American Dream.

...But wait, there's more...

Just when I thought I was off the hook of running my own business, Nathan formed a technology start-up called

EnvisionStars, where we help business owners to build positive online reputations.

A year after that, we started a dental conference business called Dental WinWin, where experts and professionals share their expertise to help dentists grow their business and clinical knowledge.

In 2020, during the COVID-19 pandemic, we started a dental supply company called DentalMedPPE, after Nathan and his colleagues had difficulty finding personal protection equipment to run their dental offices.

You might understand now that, if you are like me, married to an entrepreneur, entrepreneurs never run out of ideas.

Part of being an entrepreneur is that the list of things to do never ends. Have you heard the saying that "the best ideas come in the shower"? Yes, there is such a thing!

It got to the point that I told Nathan that if he kept pitching me with more ideas, I would forbid him from taking a shower, literally. All kidding set aside, I do want to be supportive and do not want to be a dream-crusher. I understand that new challenges are good for personal growth, but you have to say enough is enough at some point. That brings us back to our personal goals. Our goal is simple: be successful not only for our family but also to help others around the world and leave a legacy.

Nathan and I both came from low-income families. When my family settled in Texas, all we had were a few suitcases and $300 in our pockets. In the first few years, we shared a small two-bedroom apartment with another lady to cut costs. We bought our winter clothes from Goodwill and garage sales. I paid fifteen dollars for my first personal computer at a garage sale; luckily, it lasted me until college.

My parents made minimum wage. We only had one car, which occasionally would not start. Both of my parents took the night shift so my dad could drop us off and pick us up from school and work. I worked part-time throughout high school and college to help with bills and pay for my tuition. I did receive financial aid in college, but it was not enough to pay for books and tuition because I always took more classes than was required.

On the other hand, Nathan's family of seven came to Texas with couple of suitcases and no money. Just like my parents, both of his parents worked long hours and made minimum wage. His sister often worked two jobs making minimum wage to help with the bills and household expenses. During college his car often broke down at red lights and gas stations. No racing car, nor expensive stuff!

Because of our backgrounds, we both value perseverance, hard work, and the opportunity that this country has offered us; that's why sometimes it is hard to turn down opportunities.

Have you ever thought about your legacy? We hadn't until a couple of years ago when we attended a mastermind hosted by Dr. David Phelps. His question struck me: "what happens if you die tomorrow?"

It was like a wake-up call. I mean, as a mom of two young boys, with my kid's schools and extra activities, family meal preps, my work, and the list go on, this question had never crossed my mind.

I was reminded of Dr. Stephen Covey's second habit of highly effective people: "begin with the end in mind." Only this scenario begins with the eulogy: What will people say at my funeral? How did I live my life? What marks did I leave?

Did I make an impact on anyone's life? Pretty daunting, huh?

That's where I realized that I could plan my life, too, and not just react to it. We are fortunate to have loving parents who sacrificed their lives to provide their kids a better future. For me, having happy kids, a great family, and achieving financial freedom at this stage in life is more than a blessing.

Everyone has a role model growing up: for me, it was my mom. Even though my mom isn't educated, she's a powerful and wise woman. When my dad fled communist Vietnam in 1989 to find freedom for our family, he ended up in a refugee camp in Indonesia for seven years. Not only did my mom manage to raise three of us (the oldest was 11, and I was the youngest, age 7), she was able to buy more land and build a nice house. You are probably thinking that my dad must have left us money when he left. It was the opposite. My mom used all of our family's money to pay for my dad's escape from the country by boat. What was and still is great about my mom is that she works very hard, always saves, and finds opportunities to reinvest. I think I got my "money traits" from her.

What I have realized over the years is that moms play a big role in the family. Whether being a career woman, an entrepreneur's wife, or a stay-at-home mom, we tend to be in charge of managing household finances and taking care of the kids. Each one of us is unique in our way. We have to trust our guts, and at other times, we have to take that leap of faith. It's important that we have clear priorities, realize that we could do it all, but understand the power of delegation and the ability to seek others when it is needed. Burn-out is inevitable, so it's okay to take a break, rest, and reflect on what worked and what didn't. Be open-minded and always be on the lookout; one can learn valuable life lessons from people around us.

Furthermore, it's easy to wrap ourselves up in our daily activities and forget to care for ourselves. Take a moment now to acknowledge that we all need to be healthy to care for others. Life is hard enough, so let's be intentional about it, and remember that sometimes you are simply enough "as you are."

QUYEN LE

Quyen Le is a real estate investor, certified public accountant, mom of two amazing boys, and spouse of Dr. Nathan Ho, who runs two dental practices in Texas. She is the co-founder of EnvisionStars, helping business owners grow their business through online reputations. She is also the co-founder of DentalMedPPE.com, a dental supply company. She's a co-host of the Dental WinWin Summit, a dental business development program where experts and professionals share their expertise to help dentists grow their business and clinical knowledge. Quyen is passionate about business development and real estate investing. She loves to empower moms worldwide to achieve their financial freedom so that they can have more time with their families.

If we share the same values or if any of our products can help you grow your business, let's connect! You can find me on Facebook @ facebook.com/**quyen.lecpa.1**

CHAPTER 9

INNOVATIONS FOR GLOBAL IMPACT

Krystylle Richardson

How exciting it is to share on three of my favorite topics: Innovation. Leadership. Money.

Innovation is the art of making something better. In healthcare, people all over the world are creating new methods, coming up with new ideas, new and improved products each and every day. It has been my honor and my pleasure to be one of those people internationally for the past 40 years.

> *"Your journey is the precursor to your impact. Never look back and ask why. Rather, look forward and ask, how can I use my journey to create the impact, time freedom, mindset freedom, and financial freedom that I desire? Journey well and utilize the journey well."*
>
> **Krystylle Richardson**, *International Healthcare Exec, Wealth Innovation Strategist*

My journey started out in the automotive sector, coming from the land of Flint, Michigan and going to engineering school in Detroit. After spending a portion of my high school years and all of my college years in automotive, I needed a change. Upon graduation, I had numerous offers from automotive companies to continue on in engineering.

I chose to go a different route and worked in engineering at Pepsi for one year before transitioning to healthcare. My healthcare journey has taken me all over the world professionally, as well as on my own with our non-profits, Full Color Movement International and TeleHealth United. My overarching movement is called LIFE INNOVATION. There are seven pillars in that movement, and health innovation is one of the main ones.

I still consult heavily in this space as well as help women to seek and live a life of impact with my BuildThatBiz and Women-Weekendpreneur ™ initiatives. I help both women and men to specifically define their life purpose in a way that can be translated into educational talks to build their confidence and their businesses with an elite invite-only media mastery event called the Emerge Media Experience.

At the time of writing this, we have an upcoming Emerge Media Experience to be held in a castle in California, and we will be expanding to various other castles across the country and other countries in the near future.

Why am I mentioning this other part of my business? The answer is simple and is connected to what I do for healthcare innovation. The reason is that without good health, we cannot have the strength or energy to do anything else in life. The Life Innovation movement is one that is near and dear to my heart because it has helped me to see how everything we do is interconnected. This is what I teach others. You see, as an international corporate executive in some pretty large institutions, as well as smaller companies, I have found one thing to be true: Without good health it is difficult to focus on the rest of what you want out of life.

I love the term health innovation and also love discussing how I have used it throughout my journeys to create and improve many aspects of healthcare leadership, design, processes, troubleshooting, global thinking, and give-back models during medical missions. I also love to talk about innovation regarding our kindness index and how that has a direct correlation to our health. In the next portions of this chapter, we will take a deeper look at several of the pillars of LIFE INNOVATION. We will also look at a few examples on how you as the reader, can utilize innovation to improve your personal various areas of your life, profits and business.

For purposes of this chapter, we will utilize my trademarked term of Innovaligy ™, which means the study of the intricacies of the characteristics of the philosophies of innovation.

Leadership

Innovaligy™ 1: Innovation In Leading Leaders

"Leadership breeding is a choice. Excellent leaders can birth excellent leaders as long as they chose to look beyond inferiority complexes and competition. Excellent leaders look into the eyes of an impactful future. Let's all strive to have those eyes."

Krystylle Richardson, *International Healthcare Exec, Wealth Innovation Strategist*

It is a well-known fact that none of us got to where we are by ourselves. Sometimes we hear people praise their mentors and coaches and people that gave them a chance. Other times not so much. In all that we do I feel it's very important to be grateful for those who gave us hints big and small on how we should show up.

In the healthcare field, the possibilities of where we show up seem to be endless. However, out of the 40 years that I have been in industry overall this big world seems to get smaller and smaller. I started out in the automotive industry in Flint, Michigan as a high school intern. I stayed on with General Motors to work my way through school. After I graduated college, I received a number of offers from various automotive industry divisions, as well as one from Pepsi Cola. I had been in automotive for the last six years as I worked my way through school so I wanted to try something new, so I ventured off to be an engineer for Pepsi.

After one year with Pepsi to the day, I decided to look into the medical field. I saw one company that caught my eye in Gary, Indiana. It was an engineering position at a medical device company. I went for the interview and discussed all of what I had done at General Motors and Ford. Part of what I did was engineering but I also did some supervision and manufacturing improvements at one of the manufacturing and warehousing locations outside of Detroit, Michigan. Based on what I said I caught the attention of the management team at that medical company. Two weeks after the interview for the engineering position, the quality manager of the company resigned. That left an opening in management right away, even though I had interviewed for the engineering position. I was offered the manager's position due to my supervisory experience in automotive. This began a great career for me in healthcare. The person I was working for was named Harry. He was a very seasoned and approachable quality and regulatory professional.

It was Harry who became my first mentor in healthcare. For some reason, a lot of things happened in two-week time frames at that company. I mentioned earlier that two weeks after my interview for the engineering position the quality manager quit. That is when I was offered the quality manager position. Two weeks after entering the company, the FDA showed up for an unannounced inspection of our quality management system. Since I had only been at the company for two weeks Harry handled most of the inspection, but he threw me in there to gain the experience as well. I landed on both of my feet and did very well answering a number of the questions, taking tons of notes, being the person that had to go and get some of the records from the rest of the organization, while Harry continued discussions with the inspector.

Having that FDA inspection happen right when I first joined the organization probably was the best thing that could have ever happened. We ended up getting one finding on the 483, (this is the form that is used to record findings during an FDA inspection). Even though that was about 30 years ago I still remember it like yesterday. The one thing that they found was in relation to a complaint record.

After the inspection was over, we went through every single complaint that we had, and there were no other issues found. They then began to talk about what is called the inspector's touch. That means that a good inspector can find the one issue meaning the one needle in the haystack. Little did I know just going to get the documents during the inspection, taking notes, and learning the ins and outs of an FDA inspection, would have such a great impact on my career. What was happening is that I was being led by a leader. I was being groomed by a leader to be a leader.

I came into the organization thinking I was going to be an engineer, but because of previous experience, I was the first person of color in management at that particular company. Being located in Gary, Indiana, which is about one hour outside of Chicago, meant that there were a lot of people of color and from other countries that worked in manufacturing. It was a melting pot of sorts. What I also there was that a lot of women, whether it was in the break room or in the restroom or in the hallway, would always smile at me. They were very proud to see a woman in management. Some were also proud to see a woman of color in management. I then began to have people even stop me and talk to me about things that were happening in manufacturing. Some of those beautifully-hearted women would just say that they were proud of me.

Innovaligy™ 2: Innovation in processes.

> *"A good inspection can mean the difference between stagnate financials and a robust growth strategy. Take time to prepare your companies for excellent compliance. Use your results as a carrot to entice prospective customers by proving your excellence."*
>
> *Krystylle Richardson, International Healthcare Exec,*
> *Wealth Innovation Strategist*

The years went by at that company and came with several more FDA inspections as well as customer audits. I started doing audits and inspections of our suppliers. All of this was due to the training and style of my supervisor, Harry. He was a very kind gentleman who liked to laugh and always had a story about anything and everything that came up during the work day. As I began to use my engineering skills related to working on process validation, software validation, and other technical items, he would always be very encouraging and open to hear my ideas.

Another thing that he would do would be to have me lead meetings, both planned and unplanned. Sometimes I would know that I was going to lead a meeting and I could prepare. Other times, for instance when the mayor of the city came, I was asked to lead a portion of the explanation of our department. I had not prepared anything and so I was put on the spot. With the president of the company standing there, as well as Harry and other dignitaries from the city, I began to give the explanation of what we did in the quality and regulatory area. Everyone smiled and said thank you and later on I got a number of compliments from people on how well I did.

Part of being a leader of leaders is to develop them for all different types of scenarios. There are a number of other stories related to Harry and how he led. As I began to walk into other positions in other medical device companies, genetic research companies, vendors and suppliers all over the world, I saw myself using some of the techniques that I was taught by Harry. It was not necessarily called mentorship back in the 90s. He did not state that he was mentoring me, but that is what was happening.

As I continued my career in other larger companies, including GE healthcare, the leadership expectations were heightened. As a leader you are also expected to lead those that work for you in a way that helps them to be the best leaders as well. I was the global director of quality and regulatory for ultrasound probes. I had seven countries under me. This meant that I had people in management in their respective teams that I was responsible for managing. The countries included China, Japan, Norway, Austria, India, France and the United States.

Global Leadership is very different from domestic. I encourage everyone to broaden their reach and the reach of their teams to understand global thinking. I actually teach a course on it as part of Echelon Leadership Institute. That is the program that I created for junior high, high school, and college students to help them with leadership, science, technology, engineering, wealth innovation, public speaking, the importance of good troubleshooting skills, how to use their minds to create, and more. My special guests and I train on a number of tools and techniques that are not taught in the regular school system.

Some people have been said to be born a leader. Other people need help. In both cases being a good leader takes commitment. Some people have good oration skills. Some people have the ability to convince people to do anything they want. Other people have a great skill in collaboration and helping people work as a team. Being a good leader has more to do with being a good listener, and motivator of your team to take action. It has less to do with being in front.

It really makes me feel good when people that I've mentored are being creative and solving problems as a result of using techniques from our sessions. For example, I have one client that makes orthopedic implants. They are now at the point where I can check on them once or twice a year to see how things are going. Every year that I go to do their compliance audit, I am almost brought to tears. Those are good tears, by the way. The systems and techniques that they've implemented based on my mentorship and guidance are working very well. Listening to their answers to compliance questions as we get ready for the possibility of another FDA inspection is wonderful.

As a mentor I've had people that I have poured into that I was not quite sure whether they were listening or not. Then there are other times, as with this particular orthopedic company, where there is evidence that they were listening. They have grown into such great leaders. I'm very proud to see young people doing so well to make a difference in the world. In this case they are making people's lives better with great orthopedic solutions.

It is not about being up in front as a leader. It is about building leadership in those around you. I cannot wait to see how their careers will blossom based on this foundation. I'm very honored to have been a part of that foundation. I appreciate Harry doing that for me and I appreciate being able to do that for others.

Design

Innovaligy™ 3: Innovation In Design From An Innovative Mind

> *"Let us design a world that is innovative enough that all minds think of "issues" as positive growth opportunities waiting to be explored. Great leaders infuse this mindset into their teams daily."*
>
> **Krystylle Richardson**, *International Healthcare Exec, Wealth Innovation Strategist*

The word innovation in itself means that we're using things that already exist to make things better. I love using my creativity in everything I do. I teach dance and love to choreograph pieces to all different types of music. I also teach music and have written over 100 songs, some of which are published and used by various churches, singing groups, business/leadership songs, and even for media commercials.

One of the most recent songs I wrote was for a good friend of mine who passed away. His name was Frank Shankwitz. He was one of the founders of the Make-A-Wish foundation. The song can be found on YouTube and it is called "I Miss You, Hero by Krystylle Richardson." He loved cowboy hats (I do, too!) and he lived about an hour and a half from me. Whenever I travelled up his way, I would let him know I was in the area and we would have a quick conversation. I was also the red-carpet interviewer, the Red-Carpet Empress, for his movie "The Wish Man." I was at the premiere of his movie in Arizona as well as in Hollywood. He had been on my radio show a number of times as well as attending other events. He was my cowboy hat buddy. Miss him dearly.

Another thing I like to create is fashion design and I have made a number of the outfits that I wear. I've been asked to make someone's wedding dress because of something they saw that I made. Maybe years down the line I will have a fashion line, but that is not my focus right now.

One of my sketches was also hung in a dentist's office. It was a picture of a lion that had a broken tooth and was looking sad. He was holding his tail over his shoulder. How I thought of that I'm really not sure, but creativity is like that. Sometimes you're not sure where the ideas come from.

I mentioned all of these examples to bring us to design in healthcare. You see, when a person has a creative mind, the ability to imagine, and the ability to express; that is a person that you want on your design team. In healthcare, the area of design is often called Research and Development (R&D). Every company needs to have people that are always thinking about the next thing.

These are people who wake up each day thinking about the next big idea, the next new approach, the next process improvement, the next next. In a lot of areas of my life, I am this way. Always thinking, always seeing what I can do to make something better, easier, faster, cheaper, more robust, and more impactful. Everyone should have people in their company that are always looking for how they can keep the company moving toward current technology and creating the next technology. When we have parent consults or during commencement ceremonies, I always talk to parents about encouraging their child's creative thinking.

As leaders in healthcare, we should do the same. I'm responsible for quality and regulatory for various companies. There are rules, regulations and guidelines. There are templates, procedures, work instructions, forms and more. With all of that it is also important to still have ways that the employees can be creative, be spontaneous, have time with no guidelines to create, troubleshoot, brainstorm. There are various six sigma techniques that help with this as well. The point is that procedures and templates are important, but companies cannot grow without allowing for the art of creativity and creative thinking to take place. This is true in our lives as individuals as well. As leaders in medicine and in any industry, we must strike a delicate balance between structure to create and freedom to be creative.

Creativity

Innovaligy™ 4:

Innovation In Creativity

> *"Creativity and innovation have no boundaries. Let's leave our mind's eye open to see the possibilities and act on them. Seeing with no action, is a waste of our existence."*
>
> **Krystylle Richardson**, *International Healthcare Exec, Wealth Innovation Strategist*

I am talking about leadership and talking about design in this section, and the same concepts hold true in life. Relationships need to have guidelines; parents need to have rules. Our mates and our children also need to have time where their brains can just be an open space for random

Think Outside the Box

thought. This is where mindfulness comes into play. It is also where people can refresh their mind and renew their mind and then have the strength and capability to fill it with complex thoughts because they took time to be refreshed. Great designs come from refreshed minds.

Innovative leadership has guidelines but knows when to step outside of those for the good of the company, and when to step back in. This is not to say that stepping outside of the guidelines is to do anything that is against FDA or International regulations. This is simply to say that people need time to create. People need space to create. People need permission to create. Let us design our days so that we have a little bit of time for ourselves for self-care, self-reflection, self-renewal and creativity.

Missions

Innovaligy™ 5: Innovation In Global Thinking

> *"Think like a leader. Think global, think giving, think outside of yourself, think impact."*
>
> **Krystylle Richardson**, *International Healthcare Exec, Wealth Innovation Strategist*

As the ICN Global Ambassador of Innovation it has been my honor and pleasure to serve many nations. The efforts of my volunteers and staff were nominated and featured as part of a specialized track during a recent prestigious HIMSS (Healthcare Information and Management Systems Society) Global Convention for our work in Ghana and other regions in Africa and the Caribbean.

If you have never been on a medical mission, it is something that should be on your bucket list in my opinion. I know that missions are not for everyone, but some things are so life-changing that you want everyone to experience them. I've been on a number of medical missions and have coordinated a number of them as well. I am an ordained minister, missionary, and evangelist. The medical missions that we have done have been combined with a ministry aspect. I have done these types of missions in Jamaica, Barbados, Bahamas, Nigeria, Senegal, Kenya, and a number of times in Ghana.

Sometimes the medical portion has such a great need that the mission takes on its own mission. This was the case the last time we went to Ghana. We had been granted the use of some telemedicine equipment to take with us on this mission. This came about because I was doing a medical device audit of the telemedicine equipment company and got into a conversation with the president of the company. During that lunch conversation, a mission of love, hope, and care was created.

Before I get into specifics about the mission, I want to just give you a few words of encouragement. I did not go to that company to have a conversation about missions: I went to that company to perform an audit of their quality management system. During that audit, one could maybe say God had other plans. We were able to help hundreds and hundreds of people based on that one conversation. The president expressed that he had other people mention taking their telemedicine equipment on missions but then later did not follow through. I let him know if he would grant the use of the equipment, I would be sure to set up whatever was needed in order to utilize the equipment on the mission. I then set up doctors here in the United States to communicate with the doctors and nurses in Ghana related to patient consultations using their telemedicine equipment. That is also when I birthed TeleHealthUnited.com.

Innovaligy™ 6: Innovation In Global Impact

"Never underestimate the power of one connection. Never underestimate the power of one conversation. Never underestimate the power of one idea. Grow your circle and your impact with by being open to every possibility and focusing efforts on those that rise to the top of impact. Good leadership starts with focus."

Krystylle Richardson, *International Healthcare Exec, Wealth Innovation Strategist*

After auditing that medical company, several months went by as we began our preparation. There were a number of things that we had to prepare here in the United States as well as consultations with the doctors in Ghana. I was in close connection with a pastor here in the United States that knew of a need in Ghana. He then put me in touch with a pastor in Ghana so that I could set up the ministry mission portion as well as the medical mission. That pastor put me in touch with several nurses and doctors who could be my team on the ground while in Ghana. As we prepared here in the states, I then went to a training session on how to use the telemedicine equipment that I was only partially familiar with because of the audit that I had just conducted. Auditing is not the same as hands-on!

With the hands-on training I was then able to take the equipment with our team and set up several medical clinics during our trip. We had intake forms created and diagrams of how we would do patient flow in our pop-up clinics. There was also an area for nurse and doctor consultations. We were told was that there would be good internet connections as well as electricity. During the mission we had several brown outs, but we were able to get right back to work with a generator until the power came back on.

One clinic started at 6:00 p.m. and was supposed to end in three to four hours. We did not finish that clinic until 6:00 a.m. the next morning. So, a three-hour clinic turned into a twelve-hour mission of caring and hope. We performed examinations, laughed, sang songs, and bonded as our blinks got longer and longer and our bodies grew weary.

We had a few heated moments when one gentleman insisted on jumping to the front of the line and everyone told him he needed to go to the back of the line. He then took out a machete. Fortunately, he just waved it in the air and went back out. When he came back in empty-handed because the pastor told him he needed to leave the machete outside, we went ahead and let him come to the beginning of the line. During his examination, he did every single thing I asked for him to do and was very cooperative. He was very thankful and had a smile on his face, and the rest of the parishioners clapped for him as he left. Apparently, they knew that he was harmless, but I surely did not. All I saw was the machete. We laughed about it and had a great time the rest of the night after he left.

Innovaligy™ 7: Innovation In A Giving Mindset

"Dear Lord, never let me forget why you have blessed me with the gifts, talents and opportunities that you have allowed. Thank you for giving me a mind to share with others domestically and in other nations. The more you give, the more I vow to continue to give."

Krystylle Richardson, *International Healthcare Exec, Wealth Innovation Strategist*

Every ministry and medical mission I have done has had its fun and interesting times. Some of those missions have been ones that we planned on having nurses come with us from the beginning. There are others that we had plans on taking supplies from the beginning. There are others, however where people hear about what we're doing and what to donate.

I had one company give us electronic microscopes that they were not using so that we could take them with us to barter for medication for the children. There were hundreds of children that we needed to see and a number of them had fevers. They had underlying conditions based on the region they were in throughout Kenya. By having those electronic microscopes, we were able to get all the medication that was prescribed after their examinations. Were we planning on taking microscopes from the beginning of that mission planning? The answer is no. Was I planning on taking the telemedicine examination stations at the beginning of the planning for the mission several years later? The answer is no.

Innovaligy™ 8: Innovation In Medical Missions

"Missions and giving back makes people feel good. Company owners and employees want to rally around things that feel good. Build a giveback component into all that you do. Not just for the purpose of feeling good, but because it is the right thing to do, and our brothers and sisters need our help. A hand-up is better than just a hand out. Give so that they can then concentrate on sustainable goals. Next, help them learn how to sustain themselves."

Krystylle Richardson, *International Healthcare Exec, Wealth Innovation Strategist*

Innovaligy™ 9: Innovation And The Kindness Index

"Without kindness there is no true impact. Without kindness profit will be short-term as it is likely built on a shallow and weak foundation. People thrive better in a kind environment."

Krystylle Richardson, *International Healthcare Exec, Wealth Innovation Strategist*

Through my professional career and through our nonprofit, I have trained and led medical and religious missions in over 30 countries. This has been as a part of our TeleHealthUnited.com humanitarian initiatives. One thing I have found all over the world is that kindness is a universal need. In industry, we should never forget the kindness index. This Innovaligy™ pillar is a key one because our success in life and in business is tied to it.

Kindness can be more important sometimes than the technology that is being evaluated. Let's look at this a bit further. When a vendor is working with a customer and there are a few quality issues, or a few things that do not exactly work the way it was intended, kindness and interpersonal skills become the next deciding factor. If the two companies have a good working relationship, good communication, easy flow of decision-making during consultations, and a smile or two and kind words, then sometimes it is settled. The two companies will continue to work together for years to come and simply work out the quality concerns and technology shortcomings. When training up the next generation of leadership, remember to include interpersonal skills as a part of the training.

Innovaligy™ 10: Innovation And The Kindness In Leader

> *"The next great leader is the one who understands the power of kindness mixed with the intellectual quest. The next great leaders will build in intentional kindness as a core value. I salute you great leader. Thank you for realizing the need."*
>
> **Krystylle Richardson**, *International Healthcare Exec, Wealth Innovation Strategist*

In conclusion, the Innovaligy™ philosophy has more components to it, and I have only shared a few in this chapter. We all have an innovative side if we just tap into it. We all know people with great potential that may need an innovation boost. That is what the philosophy of Innovaligy™ is for, to boost the creating thinking flow and unleash greatness. Greatness harnessed and packaged correctly generates wealth innovation.

Let us all continue our quest for greatness in ourselves and others as well as increase profits as part of Wealth Innovation.

Monetize

Innovaligy™ 11: Innovation And The Power Of Positive Impact

> *"Impact can start with one great idea used to make the lives of others more fulfilled."*
>
> **Krystylle Richardson**, *International Healthcare Exec, Wealth Innovation Strategist*

Our wealth in life starts with our mindset. Wealth in healthy living, wealth in good money management decisions, wealth in a sound spiritual life, wealth in being remembered as someone that mattered, had impact and did good in the world. Wealth Innovation is more than just money. It is a state of being. I hope this journey through various portions of Life Innovation and Impact has touched you to have some thoughts on how you can have greater impact in the world using your unique creativity. Women, join me as a part of Women of Impact and Innovation International, WOIII ™. Seasoned leaders are joining in phase one. We unite and bring up the next generation of leaders based on our mastermind output and mentoring plan. Also ask about our coaching programs for the Woman-Weekendpreneur ™ to understand your unique formula for time management and productivity bursts. Contact me at KrystylleRichardson. com for more information. Contact me to determine if this is a good fit for you as a summit host, mentor, mentee, or other. Let's use our minds together and positively impact the world together, leaving a legacy of multi-dimensional wealth.

KRYSTYLLE RICHARDSON

As the ICN Global Ambassador of Innovation, Krystylle Richardson is a seasoned international healthcare and genetic research executive. Krystylle has spoken, trained and led medical and religious missions in over 30 countries as part of her TeleHealthUnited.com humanitarian initiatives. Her humanitarian efforts were nominated and featured as part of a specialized track during a recent prestigious HIMSS (Healthcare Information and Management Systems Society) Global Convention for her work in Ghana and other regions of Africa and the Caribbean.

Krystylle is also a Wealth Innovation Coach, and is the energized creator of The Woman Weekend-Preneur™, a TV show host, pastor, and engineer. Krystylle uses relentless tenacity to move individuals and corporations to sustainable profitability as The JUMPOLOGIST aka The Untapped Income Coach.

Krystylle has shared in USA Today, NBC, CBS, ABC, Yahoo Finance, and Amazon Prime on how to utilize innovation to create a life of good health, the business you have dreamed of and the impact that the world needs today and every day.

Join her movements and coaching programs by finding out more at KrystylleRichardson.com.

CPSIA information can be obtained
at www.ICGtesting.com
Printed in the USA
BVHW011512051121
620551BV00016B/345

9 781637 921715